THE
# HARRY
# GLEESON

**KIERAN FAGAN'S** interest in miscarriages of justice was prompted by living close to 10 Rillington Place in London in the 1960s. At that address serial killer John Christie had lived, and also Timothy Evans, who was hanged for murders later shown to be the work of Christie. The author is a retired journalist who has worked for *The Irish Times*, *Irish Independent* and *Sunday Tribune*.

*For Alana, Anahita and Afshin*

# THE FRAMING OF
# HARRY GLEESON

## KIERAN FAGAN

The Collins Press

First published in 2015 by
The Collins Press
West Link Park
Doughcloyne
Wilton
Cork

Reprinted 2015

© Kieran Fagan 2015
Illustrations © Fiona Aryan 2015

Kieran Fagan has asserted his moral right to be identified as
the author of this work in accordance with the Irish Copyright
and Related Rights Act 2000.

All rights reserved.
The material in this publication is protected by copyright law.
Except as may be permitted by law, no part of the material
may be reproduced (including by storage in a retrieval
system) or transmitted in any form or by any means, adapted,
rented or lent without the written permission of the copyright
owners. Applications for permissions should be addressed to
the publisher.

A CIP record for this book is available from the British
Library.

Paperback ISBN: 978-1-84889-246-0
PDF eBook ISBN: 978-1-84889-907-0
EPUB eBook ISBN: 978-1-84889-908-7
Kindle ISBN: 978-1-84889-909-4

Typesetting by Carrigboy Typesetting Services
Typeset in Palatino
Printed in Poland by HussarBooks

# Contents

Harry Gleeson with some greyhounds, which were his great
passion. Courtesy Tom Gleeson

# Preface

When I first began to look into this subject, in late 2009, I thought the job involved finding out the names of those who had murdered Mary McCarthy, or Moll Carthy as she was known locally. My plan was to bring the story up to date by publishing the names of those responsible, thus exonerating Harry Gleeson, the man hanged in April 1941 for Moll McCarthy's murder. Not long after I had begun, however, I was sidetracked by another project, and when I returned to Moll's murder in late 2011, I found that my purpose had shifted: I was less focused on who had killed her. After all, an earlier writer on the subject, Marcus Bourke, though he stopped short of naming the guilty parties, had left plenty of clues pointing to their identity. The key for me became to ask other questions. Why did they do it? How did they get away with it? This book, I hope, explains how a series of overlapping events and interests caused an innocent man to be hanged.

In looking into these matters, I found that I had to ask some hard questions of those still living, and prompt the living to ask even harder questions of the dead.

Look at the bare facts: a woman was murdered and a man was hanged for her murder. Yet most of their neighbours and friends knew at the time that the evidence that pointed to Harry Gleeson being the murderer was sketchy. Others knew, or thought they knew, that he had not killed anyone. So why did so few speak up for him? And if not then, why not later? Why, in the early 1990s, when first Bill O'Connor and then Marcus Bourke had published books showing grave flaws in the murder investigation and the trial of Harry Gleeson, did people not speak out and demand that his reputation be restored?

There was, and still is, a conspiracy of silence. Moll's promiscuous relations with certain men in New Inn, County Tipperary, and beyond left many families with guilty secrets. Fear was another factor. If Harry Gleeson did not commit the murder, then those who did were still living in the community and had shown that they were not to be trifled with. So this conspiracy of silence could more accurately be described as 'a reign of terror', as Seán Delaney of the Justice for Harry Gleeson campaign group pointed out to me. However, even after all the protagonists had died, there remained little appetite for confronting the truth. All this contributed to unease in a community that knew it had looked the other way when trouble had come to a neighbour's door. There were then, as there are now, honourable exceptions, and it is to them we owe the truth.

The townland of Marlhill, close to the village of New Inn, came to the attention of the wider world following the events of Thursday, 21 November 1940, when a farm manager, out checking on sheep, found the body of a woman with gunshot wounds. That single event would enmesh the lives of ordinary people and international figures, lawyers, diplomats and international peacemakers, film-makers and novelists, and its consequences continue to engage the attention of the public to this day. This book is an attempt to disentangle the threads that came together in what was a fairly typical community in the Irish countryside, not long after the Second World War had begun. However, there are some questions to which we will never find answers.

Where people are quoted, the text is taken from the official record unless otherwise indicated. There are conflicts in evidence between 'old time' and 'new time' because some rural people did not change their clocks for daylight-saving time. These conflicts can get in the way of comprehension. Previous writers tried to adjust the text to adopt one. I have chosen not to alter the record, but to ensure that, where timing is critical to understanding what is going on, the time lapse between events is given correctly.

# 1. South Tipperary in 1940

The village of New Inn is a pleasant, quiet backwater today, less busy than it was some seventy-five years ago. Then, it was on the main Dublin-to-Cork road, about halfway between Cashel and Cahir, and had a busy garda station with a complement of four men. The girls' secondary school was a hive of activity, just across the road from a modest parish church and quiet graveyard. Vincent O'Brien had not yet begun training horses at nearby Ballydoyle, but the land was good, and many farmers prospered in the Golden Vale, some of the finest agricultural land in Western Europe. Because of war-time supply shortages, farmers were required to plant crops, although much of the land was better suited to grazing high-quality livestock, as generally happens today.

The motte (or moat, in local parlance) of Knockgraffon is an imposing man-made earthen mound, an Anglo-Norman settlement, from the twelfth or thirteenth century, which survives to this day. Nearby is Rockwell College, in the 1940s a day and boarding school for boys run by the Holy Ghost order, now co-educational, where a young Éamon de Valera taught briefly. Knockgraffon National School, scene of some of the events in this book, closed its

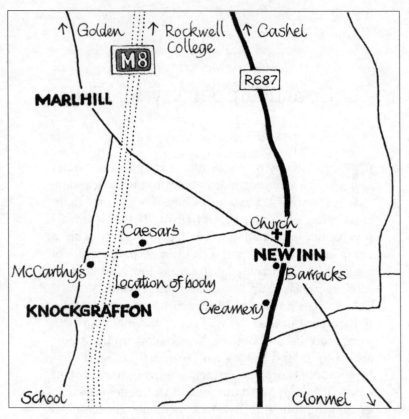

Map of the Marlhill–Knockgraffon–New Inn area today, showing M8.
COURTESY FIONA ARYAN

doors for the last time in 1992, though it outlasted New Inn Secondary School by ten years.

But a resident of New Inn from 1940 would not recognise much else about the landscape. In recent years, the M8 motorway has severed the area. The very contours of the land have changed because the motorway passes through on a raised embankment. Farmers lost many acres when the motorway was built. John Caesar's farm in the townland of Marlhill – where Mary McCarthy's body was found in November 1940 – was bisected, and what remains of it now lies on either side of the motorway, with access via a tunnel.

Caesar's land has also been combined with other adjoining farms. Many of the hedges which his farm manager maintained in 1940, and where the dead woman's children scavenged for firewood, have gone, as fields have been consolidated. A pump where the murdered woman sometimes drew water for her cottage, near the site of the demolished Caesar farm-house, remains.

The physical changes have also been more than matched by the changes in people's way of life and their attitudes. It is fair to say that in 1940 anyone who forecast that Elizabeth II, a daughter of the then reigning British monarch, would visit the nearby Rock of Cashel and be welcomed with a handshake to republican south Tipperary by a Sinn Féin mayor would have been ridiculed. Yet that is exactly what has happened.

Politically and socially, too, New Inn has changed drastically in the past seven decades. In 1940, the Easter Rising of 1916 was fresh in many memories and the atrocities of the War of Independence and the Civil War were recent events, discussed and argued over in kitchens, public houses and meeting halls.

Men who had taken up arms when they were young had become honoured members of society. Some were feared, and with good reason. Many had killed for 'the cause' and were revered for their contribution to Irish independence. Where once an Anglo-Irish aristocracy had overseen the local society, now a cohort of nationalist heroes with a claim for respect in their own locality was in charge. Many were not yet fifty, most were men, and some had been rewarded for their services with pensions from the impoverished infant state.

The presence in the community of those regarded as heroes for acts of valour in bearing arms sat uneasily alongside that of a recent creation: An Garda Síochána, the unarmed successor to the Royal Irish Constabulary. Often, if there was trouble in a neighbourhood, a word with the local IRA leader was more effective than going to the local police barracks. As I was told by a man who grew up in New Inn in the 1940s, 'They were hard, tough men; they knew how to handle guns and were not afraid to do so.'

Mary McCarthy was born around 1902 and was approaching forty years of age when she was murdered. When she was about nineteen, and working as a domestic servant in the New Inn area, she gave birth to her first daughter, Mary. The nineteen-year-old Mary McCarthy's grandfather was Edmond McCarthy. He was the second head gardener at Garranlea, home of the wealthy landowning Cooney family. He leased a cottage from them and lived there with his family.

Some time later – on the same day that Abraham Slattery bought what would become the Caesar farm from John Cooney at public auction – Edmond McCarthy bought the leased cottage, along with two acres, in which his daughter Mary and granddaughter Moll subsequently lived. His daughter, Moll's mother

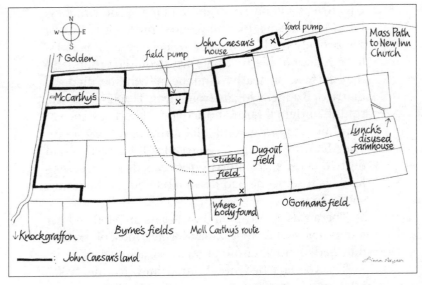

Map of John Caesar's land showing Moll McCarthy's route. COURTESY
FIONA ARYAN

(who was also called Mary), was born on 12 January
1870, the youngest of his three children. Edmond's
wife died and he remarried. When Moll's mother
Mary was thirteen, she hit her stepmother in the face
with a poker during an argument and her father
threw her out of the house. We do not know if or
when father and daughter were reconciled, but she
did inherit his cottage. She had spent some time in an
orphanage in Clonmel. When she left, she was
penniless and that, it appears, is what made her take
to prostitution, as did her daughter Moll.

Some time in the mid-1920s a farmer called John
Caesar bought the seventy-acre farm that Slattery had
acquired from John Cooney. Caesar had gone to

America as a young man and had made some money. Local legend says that he worked on the building of the Brooklyn Bridge in New York. Caesar was not a local man, but his first wife was from New Inn, and they farmed at nearby Graigue. When she died, he married Bridget Hogan from near Tipperary town, sold the original farm and moved a short distance to Marlhill, acquiring Moll McCarthy as a neighbour. The McCarthy cottage – some called it a hovel – stood on two acres surrounded on three sides by Caesar's land, as if someone had taken a bite out of the farm's southern flank.

There was no escaping the Caesars for Moll and her family: even when they wanted water, most of the time they had to draw it from pumps on Caesar's land.

The Caesars had no children and, by the 1930s, John was in his seventies, but his nephew, one of many, had joined them and worked the farm, in the expectation of one day inheriting it. This nephew was Harry Gleeson. He and Moll were about the same age.

After Moll's first child, Mary, was born, there were three Mary McCarthys living in the two-roomed cottage, soon joined by Moll's second child, Patrick, the result of her liaison with a local man, Patrick Byrne of Knockgraffon.

Moll McCarthy's mother Mary was also an un-married mother. Since Moll's father was a local man named Fitzgerald, and Moll's first child was fathered by yet another Fitzgerald, this may account for the local view that Moll's daughter Mary was, in the parlance of the time, 'a bit slow mentally'. However, as we shall see, the youngest Mary McCarthy was not mentally impaired at all. She had inherited her

mother's flaming red hair, though she was not considered to be as pretty as her mother; a local woman
who knew her as a child described her as 'dumpy'.

In the 1920s, the oldest living Mary and her
daughter Moll kept goats for breeding purposes,
as well as a greyhound and some donkeys. The
depredations caused to their neighbours' property by
wandering goats mattered little compared to the
outrage at Moll's way of life, giving birth to children
by local men, some of whom were married to, or
would later marry, 'respectable' local women.

In 1926, when Moll's mother was still living with
her, the two women and Moll's two children, Mary
and Patrick, were fortunate to escape with their lives
when the thatched roof of the cottage was set on fire.
A vacant cottage nearby was also burned – lest the
McCarthys move into it. It was clearly arson and the
McCarthys were awarded £25 in state compensation,
a considerable sum at the time.

This outrageous act, which could have caused the
deaths of four people, was blamed on local men,
acting, it was thought, on the prompting of their
womenfolk. Then it was the women's turn to disgrace
themselves. They approached the parish priest, Father
Edward Murphy, prompting him to condemn Moll
McCarthy and her way of life from the pulpit in New
Inn. We do not have a record of his remarks, though
we know she was in church to hear them. There is no
record of whether or not he also condemned the arson
attack and attempted murder visited on these
members of his flock.

Matters improved somewhat with the appointment
of a new parish priest in 1932. Father James O'Malley

appeared to be a more tolerant and easy-going man. He had served in New Zealand, and, initially, did not act upon calls from the respectable women of New Inn to do something about Moll and her increasing brood.

Matters were not helped by Moll brazenly sending her children to Knockgraffon National School where they sat in desks alongside the legitimate offspring of their various fathers. The two eldest – Mary and Patrick – enrolled on the same day, 23 April 1929. The next child, Michael, enrolled on 4 September 1933, and Ellen (known as Nellie) entered the school on 19 June 1936. When classes ended for the day, the good wives of New Inn and the surrounding area would sometimes look closely at Moll's children as they left, seeking to identify family likenesses to their husbands, brothers and even fathers.

On one occasion Moll got annoyed with this, and provoked a scene outside the school, shouting at the women to look as much as they liked, that her children were every bit as good as theirs, and saying, 'Don't they have the same fathers?' Her logic was unassailable but did not endear Moll to her neighbours.

On another occasion, Moll broke up a fight between either Patrick or Michael and another pupil, telling her son not to be hurting his brother.

When Knockgraffon National School closed its doors in 1992, a nicely produced commemorative booklet issued at the time made no mention of these excitements, but one contributor did remember the less well-off. 'We, the girls, never played with the cottage children. Thinking back on it, wasn't it

An undated photograph of Anastasia Cooney.
COURTESY CARMEL O'LEARY

disgraceful? As though being poor was not enough, without being looked down on for it?'[1]

Moll and her brood were not completely without friends. Anastasia Cooney, a daughter of the wealthy landowning family, lived nearby at Garranlea House. An unmarried and formidable woman, Anastasia had driven a battlefield ambulance during the First World War.[2] She was trained at the Mary Wardell Hospital in Stanmore, north of London, before being sent overseas. A devout Catholic, and a pillar of the local branch of the Legion of Mary, Anastasia Cooney was able to distinguish between the sinner and the sin. She befriended Moll, and let it be known that the McCarthy family had her protection. This meant that the ability of the New Inn parish priest, Father Murphy or O'Malley, to deal with the 'scarlet woman' on his doorstep was limited, since he could not afford to make an enemy of a daughter of the local Big House.

However, Anastasia Cooney was the only 'respectable' local woman known to have crossed the door of Moll McCarthy's cottage, and she acted as godmother for some of Moll's children. She also arranged for the burial of Moll's seventh and last child, Margaret, known as Peggy, who lived for only about three weeks. Anastasia herself is laid to rest in a Cooney plot in Kilsheelan on the Tipperary–Waterford border, which is also where she had baby Peggy buried.[3]

But as Moll's family grew, staff at nearby Rockwell College saw to it that surplus food from the boarding school kitchen found its way to her cottage. She also received a payment of six shillings a week from the local welfare officer, who paid for her to receive a daily pint of milk from a local farmer, John Condon. The manager of the adjoining farm, where Moll used to go to draw water, also gave her an occasional bag of potatoes. His name was Harry Gleeson.

## 2. A Wicked Murder

In the early half of the twentieth century, market day was an important event in the life of any rural town and for those who lived in surrounding areas, much more so than it is today. The daily routine of the farm was disrupted as the fattened animals were prepared for the journey, before the farmer and his wife, sometimes farmhands too, set off for a day of bargaining, meeting old friends and hoping for a good price for their livestock and produce. The farmer looked forward to a few pints when the negotiations were finished, while the women caught up with local news and saw what new goods the shops had to offer. Market day was a big event that involved many changes and distractions from day-to-day life in rural Ireland – and these distractions also made it a good opportunity to prepare for a murder.

When Michael Harris's hired lorry drove into Caesar's farmyard on the morning of Wednesday, 20 November 1940, to collect pigs to take to the fair in Cashel, John Caesar came out to help load the animals. He then got into the cab of the lorry beside Harris and they set off for Cashel, then a market town of some 3,000 people. Bridget Caesar would follow her husband later in the pony and trap. Unlike today's dedicated marts on the outskirts of large towns, in the

1940s the market took place on the streets, and shop owners put screens outside windows to protect them from animals lurching in through the glass.

While the farmers haggled and bargained, the women sold their eggs, vegetables and other produce to the local grocer. And this is how it was for Bridget Caesar, who then bought what she needed for the coming month – tea, sugar, paraffin oil, soap and candles, and perhaps something new to wear for Christmas.

On that particular fair day in November 1940, after all the bargaining had been done, John Caesar was ready for a pint. There was no shortage of watering holes in Cashel and while he enjoyed a drink in one of the public houses where men were gathered, his wife took a small glass of port in the snug of Ryan's Hotel at the top of the town. Those with more robust republican views frequented Davern's bar in Main Street, a family-run business with strong IRA and Fianna Fáil connections.[1]

Later in the afternoon, the Caesars returned home in the pony and trap, full of talk of the day's doings and the price they had got from a man called Cantwell who had bought their pigs. Tommy Reid and Harry Gleeson, who had stayed behind to work the farm, would want to know all the details. According to her son Michael, their neighbour Moll McCarthy saw the Caesars' pony and trap returning up the road past her cottage.

That day Harry Gleeson had been ploughing the stubble field a few minutes' walk away from the Caesar farmhouse. When the light started to fade, which was also around the time the Caesars were setting out on their journey home, he decided to call it a day. The field was partly tilled and partly pasture, and sheep were grazing on the pasture side. He returned to the farmyard and began to feed the cattle and settle them down for the night. Tommy Reid, the farmhand – he got paid for his work, unlike Harry Gleeson, who hoped to inherit the farm and so was paid no wages, having to subsist on what he earned from training greyhounds for coursing matches, and other odd jobs – helped him to clear up after the day's work. They were both tired following the early start to the day loading up the pigs to send them to market.

Moll McCarthy was not what most people, in New Inn or elsewhere, would have described as an ideal neighbour. She had been a very pretty young woman, with striking red hair and good features, and, by 1940, even though she was fading slightly into middle age, men still found her attractive. So much so that she had given birth to six children by different men from the general locality and, earlier that year, a seventh child, a little girl, had died a few weeks after birth.

Life was hard in Moll's cottage. At one time, it had been thatched, but by 1940 it had been reroofed with corrugated iron, making it more difficult to heat. For fuel, the family depended largely on collecting twigs and cuttings from hedges and trees in the locality. This inevitably brought them into conflict with neighbours, who saw the children pulling branches off trees and bushes in hedgerows that were essential to stop their cattle from straying. Good fences make good neighbours, as the poet Robert Frost noted, and scavenging for fuel had the opposite effect. To make things worse, Moll kept goats, which would

Moll McCarthy's cottage. COURTESY NATIONAL ARCHIVES

often escape and eat everything in sight. None of this endeared the McCarthys to their neighbours.

Of Moll's six children, the two eldest had left school. Mary, who was eighteen, had been working as a live-in maid at a nearby house, but had returned home recently following a dispute over unpaid wages. Patrick was fifteen and worked for a local farmer called Hanley. He slept at Hanley's farm, but he came home most evenings after work for a few hours. The next child was twelve-year-old Michael, who, in 1940, fitfully attended the local national school at Knockgraffon, along with his sister Nellie. The two youngest children, Bridget and Connie

(Cornelius), were still at home. As a family, they seemed to get along well, despite their poverty and humble abode.

In the early evening on that November day in 1940, as John and Bridget Caesar were sitting down to their evening meal, around the same time, just a few hundred yards away, Moll was getting ready to go out. Five of Moll's children were in or around their home when she left some time after 5.30 p.m.; Patrick would come from work later. Michael and Nellie had gone to a nearby house to collect milk and a payment for the servicing of a female goat by Moll's billy goat. A garda sergeant had called to the cottage earlier, at around 3.30 p.m. Some said he had a summons to serve on Moll because the children had not been attending school; others said he wanted to have sex with her – and either account or both may have been correct. Exactly why Sergeant Anthony Daly visited Moll that day has never been satisfactorily explained. At the time he was living in the garda station in New Inn because he was relatively new in the neighbourhood and his wife had not yet joined him.

Not long after the Caesars ate their evening meal together, Moll McCarthy was taking a shortcut across the Caesar farm in the direction of the village of New Inn. She was dressed to go out, though she did not tell her children where she was going, and the path she took brought her to the stubble field in which Harry had been working earlier in the afternoon. Her dress was simple enough – she had little to spend on clothes, and she was wearing odd shoes. Darkness was falling fast.

Her route across the field led to another popular shortcut to New Inn – known as the Mass Path – which ran along the side of Caesar's farmhouse.

What we do know is that after Moll left her cottage that evening, nobody would admit to seeing her alive again.

Just down the road from Moll's cottage, a card game would soon begin at the home of Frank Lenehan and his wife. They were hosting a regular 'gamble', a card game for which the prize was a pair of chickens. Their little pebble-dashed cottage – a half-mile south of Moll's cottage – was packed for the evening and the children were told to stay in their bedroom. Peter, one of those children, who was twelve years old at the time, remembers the names of many who were present.[2] Farmers James Condon, John Halpin and Willie Fitzgerald were present. Ned Clifford was also there, and so were Johnny and Jimmy McGrath, cousins of the Lenehans. The absence of four regular participants at the 'gamble' was also noted, certainly by the older Lenehan children, and very likely by others, too. Thomas Hennessy, Jack 'The Boss' Nagle, Patrick J. O'Gorman ('Pak' Gorman) and Patrick or Paddy Byrne were all missing, and all lived in close proximity to Moll's cottage. Thomas Hennessy would later say in evidence that he had gone to Cahir that evening.

On his way home from work, Frank Lenehan had cycled down the road past Moll's cottage at about 6.15 p.m., but had noticed nothing out of place.

There are two versions of what happened to Moll after she left her cottage. One says that she and an unknown man had sex in a nearby disused dwelling, known as Lynch's farmhouse, and that sometime later she was killed instantly by a shot that severed her carotid artery. Nobody knows for certain whom she went to meet that evening, but if she had arranged to meet just one man, others had to have joined him. Had one person carried the body, the pathologist's report would have noted markings caused in transit.

We do know that Moll's body did not lie in the field all night. Her clothes would have been sodden with rain. The body was probably moved just before daylight. Another shot, fired from a shotgun, was fired at Moll McCarthy's dead body – most likely as she lay in the field where she was found – and it took away her face.

The second theory, which came from the police, is that the man she went to meet was Harry Gleeson. Some time around 6 p.m., he slipped out of the Caesar farmhouse, intercepted Moll or met her by arrangement, shot her twice and left her body overnight in the stubble field. According to the police's theory, there was nobody else involved. Thomas Hennessy said he had heard shots coming from the direction of the Caesar farm around at that time, and the police took this as confirmation of their version of events.

The next thing we definitely know is that, later in the evening when his mother did not return, Patrick, Moll's eldest son, became concerned and went out with a dog and a lamp to look for her. He checked around Caesar's farm, including the stubble field where his mother's body was found the next day, but did not find anything. He decided not to return to Hanley's farm where he worked, instead staying with his brothers and sisters that night in the hope that their mother would come home, but she was still not back when he set off for work the following morning.

The next day, Thursday, 21 November, Harry Gleeson was out looking for his uncle's bull and sheep sometime around 9.30 a.m. when he saw a body lying near a hedge in a corner of the stubble field. He later said that a small barking dog was crouched on the body, obscuring his view of the victim's head, and so he did not recognise Moll. He went first to tell his uncle John Caesar and his wife Bridget, and then ran across the fields to the New Inn garda station to report what he had found. That probably took Gleeson about ten to fifteen minutes.

At the station, Gleeson told Garda Vincent Scully, the first person he met there, that he had come across the body of a woman. He could not go closer because Moll's little black dog was crouched on her chest and barking angrily; he had dogs with him and was afraid he would not be able to control four dogs. He never got close enough to see the woman's face, but thought she might be sleeping or even dead.

Gleeson, whose hobbies included hare-coursing, had three dogs with him that morning when he went looking for his uncle's flock of sheep. Two were Caesar's farm dogs, sheepdogs most likely, and one greyhound, which happened to belong to Garda Scully – Gleeson was training it for a coursing meeting because Scully lived in rented rooms. Scully's dog had to be put on a leash when he would not obey Harry's voice commands, as the farm dogs would. After Harry Gleeson told Scully about the woman in the field, the garda called his station sergeant, Anthony Daly, from

New Inn garda station, photographed in 2007. Courtesy Creative Commons

the living quarters above the barracks; then he, Garda Joseph Ruth and Harry Gleeson got into a garda car and went to the field where the body was lying. They approached the body from a different direction to that initially taken by Gleeson, and each of the men instantly recognised Moll McCarthy by her hair. 'Look at the foxy red head on her,' Harry Gleeson said. Even in death, with most of her face missing, Moll's flaming red hair caught the men's eyes.

Daly told Gleeson to remove the barking dog from the body and to get a sheet to cover it. Gleeson now had Moll's blood on his clothes from picking up and carrying the dog. John Caesar's farm became a crime scene. A police guard was put in place to keep people away from the corpse.

A curate, Father Denis Blackburn, came to administer the last rites and a Cashel GP, Dr James O'Connor, was summoned to examine the body, getting there shortly after 1 p.m. He could see immediately that Moll McCarthy had been shot dead. However, he did not detect that she had been shot twice – that would emerge from the state pathologist's examination the following day. Dr O'Connor did note that rigor mortis had already set in and that the body had not cooled a great deal. It was just 3 degrees Fahrenheit below normal body temperature. The doctor also deduced that the dead woman did not appear to have been in the field for long. The body was lying awkwardly, and Dr O'Connor said this suggested that it could have had been moved.

In the afternoon, Superintendent Patrick O'Mahony arrived from his headquarters in Cahir. He was the senior garda officer in the area, reporting to Chief Superintendent Edward Reynolds at divisional headquarters in Thurles. This crime was not one to leave in the hands of the complement of four men at New Inn station, Sergeant Daly and Gardaí Vincent Scully, Joseph Ruth and Frank Gralton. O'Mahony's first act was to have the body covered with a waterproof tarpaulin. He then drafted in thirty or forty gardaí to search the surrounding fields, drains and hedges. Sergeant Anthony Daly stayed at the scene for some hours before going back to New Inn garda station, though he later returned to Caesar's farm, where he picked up some discarded spent shotgun cartridges, Eley No. 4 grade.

Superintendent O'Mahony, accompanied by Detective Sergeant James Reynolds, called on John

Caesar and took from him his Harrison and Richardson single-barrelled shotgun, together with some cartridges and a cleaning rod. It seems that, at this point, the entire Caesar household was under suspicion.

Harry Gleeson and Tommy Reid continued to work on other parts of the farm, tending cattle and sheep, and repairing fences: the daily round of work that a mixed farm requires.

The next day, Friday, 22 November, Dr John McGrath, the state pathologist, arrived from Dublin in the mid-morning, around the same time as ballistics expert Superintendent Daniel Stapleton, but they travelled separately. McGrath conducted a preliminary examination in the field, then had Moll's body removed to New Inn garda station. There, he made a detailed examination with the help of Dr O'Connor. It was at this point that McGrath found that Moll had been shot twice, and had died of shock and a haemorrhage. Her skull had been fractured in several places, her jugular vein had been punctured and her spine had also been fractured. One side of her face had been blown away and pieces of bone and teeth were found near the body.

McGrath estimated the time of death as between twenty-four and forty-eight hours before he took the temperature of the body at 1.50 p.m. on that Friday. (Since Moll's body was found twenty-seven hours before Dr McGrath arrived, his conclusion does not add much to our understanding of what happened.) Dr McGrath would later say that he could not account for the relatively high body temperature recorded by Dr O'Connor – he could only offer his opinion based on his own examination. He also found about two dozen lead pellets from a shotgun on or close to Moll's body, as well as cartridge wads in her clothes and one in her hair. He said that her coat was buttoned, that there was blood on its interior and that her body had been lifted, probably to move it away from the fence so that it would be more easily seen and found. The grass and stones under her body were dry, as were her clothes, despite the rain on the Wednesday night. The dry ground would pose a significant problem for the defence, with its implication that the body had lain out all night.

After the post-mortem examination was finished, the local coroner, Dr P.J. Stokes, opened an inquest at New Inn garda station on the Friday afternoon. A jury was hastily assembled from the local population, one of whom was a retired tailor, Joseph Moloney, who will appear later in this story. At the inquest, Sergeant Daly gave evidence of last seeing Moll alive on Wednesday, 20 November at about 3.30 p.m., a few hours before she disappeared.

Garda Ruth gave evidence of going with Sergeant Daly and Harry Gleeson to where the body lay. He described approaching the body, which had a black dog lying on its chest, and said he recognised Moll McCarthy from a distance of about eight yards.

The state pathologist, Dr McGrath, then summarised his findings and said that the body had lain where it was found for 'anything up to ten hours'. (That would put the time of death at around midnight, but it conflicts with Dr O'Connor's temperature reading, which suggests a much later death.) The inquest was adjourned.

Some time after this initial inquest on the Friday, Anastasia Cooney took possession of Moll's body and had it buried. But while all this was happening, Inspector Thomas O'Reilly and Sergeant Matthew Breen, who had been drafted in by Superintendent O'Mahony, were interviewing Harry Gleeson in the sitting room of John Caesar's farmhouse. They arrived at about 4 p.m. and, seeing Gleeson in the farmyard, asked to talk to him. They did not caution him, later saying that he was not a suspect at that time. According to their version of events, Gleeson agreed to tell them about his movements over the previous days, but began by asking them if they had found out when Moll had died. O'Reilly told him that he didn't know.

The gardaí asked Gleeson to describe his movements on the previous day. Gleeson told them he got up around 8 o'clock, lit a fire and had his breakfast. Then he went to milk the cows with Tommy Reid at about 8.50 a.m., getting back to the house at 9.30 or soon after. He had then gone out to exercise a greyhound (meaning Scully's dog; the farm dogs followed him around as a matter of course), to find a straying bull and to count his uncle's sheep. He crossed a field known as the dug-out field – so-called because close to its eastern boundary there was a shallow hidden burial place where arms had been stored during the War of Independence. He got to the gap in the ditch between the dug-out field and the stubble field around 9.45 a.m. He had jumped up on the raised ditch, seen the body lying in the field and decided to go back to the house to summon help. He could not see the face of the person lying in the field because a little black dog was sitting on the chest. He explained that he did not cross the ditch into the field because he had the greyhound with him. He ran back to the house, told his uncle and aunt of his find, and then went to report what he had seen to the gardaí at New Inn.

Even allowing for the wooden style of recording statements in official language, this exchange seems to have been business-like and even friendly in places. In it, Harry Gleeson talks conversationally about Moll and his encounters with her around the fields and at the pump[3] on John Caesar's farm where she drew water, and the constant irritant of her straying goats. In his statement, Gleeson named the fathers of the six children and filled in details about their addresses and occupations, where he knew them. The identities of the fathers of six of Moll's children were well known around New Inn, Gleeson said.

In Gleeson's account, a man called Patrick Fitz- gerald of Marlhill was Mary's father; Patrick (Paddy) Byrne of Knockgraffon was the father of Patrick, the second child; Paddy Barron, who worked as a labourer at Nagle's farm in nearby Garrandee, was the father of Michael; a man called Connors, from Golden, was Nellie's father; a Rockwell College cook called Mahony was the father of Bridget; and the youngest boy, Con, had been fathered by Cornelius Kearney. Moll had spoken openly about the names of the fathers of the first six children, but had not told Gleeson who was responsible for the seventh, Margaret (Peggy), who had been born and died earlier that year.

Gleeson said he had not shot vermin in the past few weeks, nor had he heard anyone else shooting on the Wednesday and Thursday.

Three days later, on Monday, 25 November, the investigation swung into a higher gear. John and Bridget Caesar were summoned to New Inn garda station. Tommy Reid, who had earlier given Harry Gleeson an alibi for the two time slots in which the gardaí now appeared to think Gleeson might have killed Moll McCarthy, was held there separately and refused to change his statement to suit the case the gardaí were now piecing together. Gleeson was interviewed again at length after being cautioned that anything he said might be taken down in writing and used in evidence against him. There was no lawyer present.

The second questioning of Harry Gleeson took place in the Caesar's sitting room. This time, it was more of an interrogation. One of the gardaí had lit a fire: a well-known tactic to make the person being interrogated uncomfortable, according to some observers; a necessary measure on a wintry November afternoon, according to others.[4]

Be that as it may, the interrogation stretched over the course of thirteen hours, from just past midday on Monday until 1 a.m. the next day – more than five days after Moll was last seen. According to the gardaí, Harry Gleeson first insisted on asking if the time of Moll's death had been established, as he had done on the previous Friday. Again, this does not form part of either statement Gleeson signed. There was no lawyer present on that second occasion either.

Gleeson began by telling Superintendent Patrick O'Mahony and Inspector Thomas O'Reilly that he was about thirty-eight years of age and had lived and worked with his uncle John Caesar for sixteen years, first at Graigue, about half a mile from Marlhill, and later, after his uncle's first wife had died, at Marlhill. Caesar had remarried shortly after the move.

> I am not paid a wage by my uncle, but anytime I want a pound or three pounds or more, I have to get it from my uncle or his wife. I have got no promise from my uncle that I will get his farm at any time. The way things are, if my uncle and his missus were gone, I believe I would have the best right to the farm and, if I didn't get it, I would get a fair thing out of it. I have been on excellent terms with my uncle's wife since they were married. I never had a row with my uncle or his wife since they were married, just as if she were my mother.

Gleeson went on to describe the household arrangements. He, John and Bridget Caesar, and the farmhand Tommy Reid, who was about twenty-five years old, lived in the farmhouse. Gleeson was sometimes teased by his uncle about getting married. 'My aunt has a niece and she comes here on holidays sometimes and my uncle would come in from town and he would tell her to grow up and get strong and the two of us could be married, meaning I and she.'

Harry Gleeson then listed his daily round of chores on the farm: milking cows, sending milk to the dairy, feeding horses, letting them out to graze, counting sheep, ploughing fields, and endlessly trimming hedges and mending fences; and also looking for the bull, which was given to breaking out and making for the cows on neighbouring farms. When he was not working, Gleeson liked to read the sports pages of the newspapers that his neighbour John Halpin passed on to him, mainly about hare-coursing which was a big interest of Gleeson's. He trained greyhounds for coursing meetings.

Gleeson's account of his movements on the day before he found Moll McCarthy's body remained consistent from his first statement to the gardaí through to the murder trial, though Judge Martin Maguire would rebuke him at the murder trial for an error of a few minutes in his account of the morning when he had found Moll's body lying in the field.

He then told the two policemen about his movements in the hours before he found the body. The statement by Tommy Reid, who was with Gleeson for much of that time, confirmed his account. At the time Harry Gleeson was giving his statement to O'Mahony and O'Reilly, two other gardaí, one a chief superintendent, were with Tommy Reid in New Inn station trying to get him to change his evidence to deprive Harry Gleeson of an alibi.

Gleeson was questioned about his dealings with Moll McCarthy.

> I have known her since I came to this side of the county from my own home. That is about sixteen years, but I had not much recourse with her until we came to live here about thirteen or fourteen years ago. We often cut trees on the side

27

of the road near her house and I used tell her she could have the light branches … she often took branches or bushes without permission. She often got water in the pump in the pump field, and also in the pump in the house [the pump in the farmyard, adjoining Caesar's house], she always had a flock of goats and they used trespass on my uncle's land. She used to be after them. I met her frequently when she was taking away bushes, drawing water or turning out the goats. I was always friendly with her and spoke to her often – always when I met her.

Gleeson told them he had thrown a bag of potatoes over Moll's fence one evening a couple of years before, though his aunt and uncle knew nothing about it. And he gave her son Patrick apples in return for him pumping water for the Caesars, and had also paid him for trapping some rabbits.

The next question tells us where the gardaí were going with their line of questioning.

'When you were down at the pump last Tuesday, were you talking to Moll McCarthy?'

'No, sir.'

'Did you get a bag from her that day to get potatoes for her the next day while your uncle would be away?'

'No, sir.'

Gleeson then denied having made an arrangement to meet Moll McCarthy on the Wednesday evening, the day she went missing, at the dug-out field, to hand over a sack of potatoes.

The exchange shows one plank of the emerging prosecution case: Gleeson was meeting Moll at the field pump, away from prying eyes, and arranging to give her potatoes in exchange for sex. When she left home for the last time on the Wednesday evening, it was for a tryst with Gleeson, the gardaí concluded.

But this belief alone – even if it had been proved – would not be enough to convict Gleeson of murder.

The gardaí also asked him about the last time he had spoken to Moll, which he said was about three weeks before she was killed. He told them that he had asked her to remove her marauding goats and that her son Michael was with her.

Gleeson also made it quite clear that Moll had never told him who Peggy's father was, nor had she ever suggested that he himself was the father.

Meanwhile, since it was a Monday, Tommy Reid took John Caesar's milk to the creamery on the Dublin–Cork road, just outside New Inn. As Reid returned on the ass and cart, Garda Frank Gralton emerged from New Inn station to tell him that he was wanted inside to give a statement. Gralton tied up Reid's donkey, as if he knew that Reid would be in the police station for some time.

Chief Superintendent Edward Reynolds greeted Tommy Reid at the door, and he and Detective Sergeant James Reynolds (no relation) took Reid to a back room where they proceeded to interrogate him. Both men were from the divisional headquarters at Thurles. When Reid was allowed to leave thirteen hours or so later, he had a black eye and a swollen and discoloured face. Sergeant Anthony Daly, who was present in the station during the interrogation, had staunched the bleeding from Reid's nose. When Dr O'Connor examined Reid the following day, he found a 'two-inch abrasion in front of the left ear, consistent with [his] having been struck with a fist'. Father O'Malley also saw Reid in the days following the assault in the barracks and remarked on the man's injuries, saying that those responsible should not get away with what they had done.

The chief superintendent and the sergeant had administered a beating to Reid to try to get him to change that portion of his statement that gave Gleeson an alibi for the two occasions when the gardaí then thought the murder might have taken place – on the Wednesday evening or the Thursday morning. They also wanted Reid to say that Harry Gleeson had admitted to him that he was the father of Peggy, Moll's seventh child, and that Gleeson had buried the child at the little graveyard in Garranlea, adjoining the Cooney family home near New Inn. Had Reid given in and said that Gleeson had buried the child in the Cooney family burial ground at Garranlea, he might have done him a favour. That was easy to disprove because it could be shown that Anastasia Cooney had arranged for the infant's burial at Kilsheelan, beside St Mary's church, on the Tipperary–Waterford border.

Tommy Reid had first been questioned for two to three hours and then given a break and some tea and bread and butter. After lunch, the questioning resumed, with Chief Superintendent Reynolds writing down Reid's answers. At about 5.30 p.m., Garda Ruth brought in tea, and Tommy Reid was left alone for about half an hour. Then the chief superintendent resumed questioning Reid for about thirty minutes.

Close to 11 p.m., a full twelve hours after the interrogation had begun, the chief superintendent told Tommy Reid to sign the statement he had compiled. The statement covered his activities during the period from Wednesday, 20 November to Monday, 25 November 1940.

> I told him [the chief superintendent] of the work I had done, of whom I had been working with, and talking to, that I had been working at turnips with Gleeson and that I had discussed the murder with him. He asked me about the actual conversation I had with Gleeson and with the Caesars. He asked about Father Blackburn's visit [the curate who administered the last rites to Moll's body where it lay in the field], and about the gun – where it used to be kept – and about the cartridges and cleaning rod. He also asked me about Gleeson's movements and about my visit to the village on Wednesday night.

This shotgun belonged to John Caesar and the question of who had access to it would be a major issue at the murder trial.

There was then another break, during which Reid smoked a cigarette in the corridor with Garda Ruth, before he was called back into the dayroom. Chief Superintendent Reynolds told Reid to stand over by the wall and to put out the cigarette. Other policemen present in the station at that phase of the investigation included Sergeant Anthony Daly, a detective sergeant called Vaughan and an inspector named Lincoln. Tommy Reid described what followed, in a statement taken by his solicitor John Timoney in May 1941:

Chief Superintendent Reynolds then came to my right-hand side and [Detective] Sergeant Reynolds stood at my left.

'Had Harry his boots off when he called you Thursday morning?' the chief superintendent asked.

'He had.'

'Is it after coming in he was?'

'No, he was only after getting up,' I replied.

'Is it after coming in he was?' repeated the chief superintendent.

The chief superintendent then struck me with his fist on the right side of my face, saying, 'Say yes' over and over again.

One of the policemen – Reid could not recall which – then asked Reid if Gleeson was the father of Moll's seventh child. 'I never heard that,' Reid replied.

Both policemen then struck Reid, one from each side, saying, 'You know' and 'Say yes' repeatedly, while Reid protested that he did not know.

Sergeant Reynolds then asked if he knew how many children Moll had. Reid replied, 'Seven.'

There then followed an exchange about how Reid knew this, and if Garda Ruth had told him this or was it a man called Jack Delaney. The two Reynoldses left the dayroom soon after this, and Sergeant Daly wiped the blood from Reid's nose. Reid remembers Sergeant Daly saying that, 'The poor chap [Reid] knows nothing. He's quite innocent', though he could not recall if the chief superintendent was still present at the time.

Inspector Lincoln asked Reid how he knew where the seventh child was buried and continued to question Reid in a hostile fashion, writing down the answers, but not asking him to sign the record. Eventually he told Reid to gather himself and go.

Reid retrieved the donkey and cart and set out for his home, John Caesar's house. He said he knew it was after midnight, as the streetlights went out then, and two cars passed him on his journey and he thought they had been coming from the Caesars' house.

The day after Gleeson's second interrogation – a Tuesday – Superintendent O'Mahony went with Gleeson to the McCarthy cottage to see if he could locate a sack, which gardaí maintained Gleeson had earlier said was missing from a pump on Caesar's land. In O'Mahony's account, he called to the Caesars' farm and got hold of Harry Gleeson, and they both went across the fields to Moll McCarthy's cottage. O'Mahony hoped to find a missing sack that he maintained Gleeson had got from Moll the day before she was last seen. The suggestion was that she had given him an empty bag for him to fill with potatoes, and meet her at the dug-out field the following evening. There was no shred of evidence to support this supposition, so O'Mahony had to 'find' some.[5]

When O'Mahony and Gleeson arrived at the McCarthy cottage to search for the sack, Moll's sons Patrick and Michael were there, as O'Mahony had previously arranged. Superintendent O'Mahony then made notes of a conversation between Harry Gleeson and Moll's eldest sons that would become central to the prosecution's case in the murder trial. There were no other witnesses to this conversation, although another garda – a sergeant called Kelly – had gone with O'Mahony to the McCarthy home. O'Mahony later produced a 'verbatim' note of what was said, though he admitted that it was not in his official notebook in the correct date sequence.

The salient points of this alleged conversation were that Michael had said that his mother had given Gleeson a sack the day before she went missing, that Moll and Harry Gleeson had arranged to meet at the dug-out field the following day (Wednesday, 20 November 1940) to hand over the sack filled with potatoes – the implication being that this was a payment for sex – while John and Bridget Caesar were in Cashel for fair day.

Patrick accused Gleeson of being the father of Moll's last child, but Gleeson denied it. Patrick said that Gleeson often gave his mother potatoes. Gleeson denied that too. Michael said that his mother told him that Gleeson was the father of the last child. Gleeson said that his mother was a liar. There was no other witness to this conversation, although Sergeant Kelly had accompanied O'Mahony to the Caesar home. O'Mahony's full account of this exchange is reproduced in chapter three. This conversation would prove crucial in the conviction of Harry Gleeson. Moll's sons gave evidence at the beginning of the murder trial and neither mentioned this conversation, nor was either questioned about it. Gleeson denied that the exchange, as described, took place. The appeal court found this aspect of the evidence unsatisfactory, but not enough to upset the jury's verdict. Many in New Inn doubted that this conversation had ever taken place – at least not in the way that O'Mahony described it.

He did not know it, but Harry Gleeson only had four days of freedom left to him. On Saturday, 30 November, he was arrested at John Caesar's house and brought to New Inn garda station where Superintendent O'Mahony charged him with the murder of Moll McCarthy. Nine days had passed since he had found the body.

When answering the charge, Gleeson replied that he had 'neither hand, act nor part' in the murder and asked when the crime had been committed. The answer – 'between 5 p.m. on Wednesday November $20^{th}$ and 10.20 a.m. on Thursday $21^{st}$' – left him none the wiser.

At a special court sitting in Cashel garda station a little later, a peace commissioner remanded Gleeson to appear at Fethard District Court in five days. He was then taken the forty miles to Limerick Jail.

Harry Gleeson had no legal representation, so Bridget Caesar sent for John Timoney, a solicitor based in Tipperary town. Timoney was a friend of the Caesars and a first cousin of Dolly Furlong, whose husband Pat was a close friend of Harry Gleeson and had played hurling with him for Rockwell Rovers. The Furlong family in New Inn were among the few people to stand up for Harry Gleeson then and later. Some forty years later, Tim Godfrey, a cousin of Pat Furlong's, made strenuous efforts to help clear Gleeson's name, following publication of Marcus Bourke's *Murder at Marlhill* in 1993.

Superintendent O'Mahony did not take the news of Timoney's involvement very well. Timoney was in the habit of defending people for whom O'Mahony had little time. John Caesar and John Timoney set out on Monday, 2 December to visit Harry Gleeson in Limerick Jail. The purpose of the visit was for Timoney to meet Gleeson and be formally appointed to defend him.

O'Mahony knew that Bridget Caesar would be alone, so he called to see her. He wanted to know why she did not engage a local solicitor and asked if Timoney had come looking for the case. Timoney's office was twenty miles away, a considerable distance in 1940s' Ireland. O'Mahony suggested that the Caesars should use Maher and Co. of Cashel. Bridget Caesar countered by asking why Tommy Reid had been beaten up for telling the truth in New Inn garda station. O'Mahony, according to Bridget Caesar, replied that sometimes 'you have to beat out of a fellow what's in him'.

A few days later, Inspector O'Reilly, Detective Sergeant Vaughan, who had been present when Tommy Reid was questioned in New Inn station, and Garda Scully made a similar suggestion to Pat Furlong about getting a local man to represent Gleeson. Furlong, a local farmer, was not a man to be trifled with; he was revered locally for being a member of one of the Tipperary teams that had won a 'Triple Crown' of three All-Ireland titles in 1930. Furlong alerted Mrs Caesar, who told Timoney. Timoney drove to Cahir garda station to complain about the police trying to influence the defendant's choice of legal representation.

But, by then, Timoney was also representing Tommy Reid in his case against the two gardaí for assault, so the battle lines had been twice drawn between the gardaí and Gleeson's defence team.

On 6 December 1940, Timoney challenged Chief Superintendent Reynolds over the beating of Tommy Reid. Timoney did not know then that he was speaking to the ringleader. Reynolds told him that if anything illegal had happened, it would be dealt with, not covered up. Reynolds admitted to Timoney that Detective Sergeant Vaughan had recently been accused of mistreating a witness. Reynolds also told Timoney of another case in which a complainant had dropped a charge because he believed the guilty policemen would perjure themselves. Was this a warning of what was to come?

This exchange took place outside Fethard courthouse. Inside, District Justice Seán Troy remanded Harry Gleeson in custody until 19 December. Timoney went to Dublin on 9 December to meet barrister Seán MacBride, who had stepped down as chief of staff of the IRA in 1937, and who accepted a brief to act as junior counsel for Gleeson. The senior counsel would be the more experienced James Nolan-Whelan. Timoney may have wanted MacBride as junior counsel because of his growing reputation for winning difficult cases. Superficially, the choice was an odd one politically because the Timoney family had been Cumann na nGaedheal/Fine Gael supporters, but as historian Dr Denis Marnane explained: 'I imagine that, like many people from a traditional pro-Treaty background, Timoney was fed up with Fine Gael and, like others, was enraptured by the glow of MacBride's charisma that seemed to promise a "new politics".'[6]

Local sources have suggested that John Caesar was a 'Blueshirt' and had been known to appear in the militia uniform. I have not been able to substantiate this, but it seems likely that he had supported the pro-Treaty side in the Civil War, and this would have separated him from his instinctively more republican-leaning neighbours. Timoney's own politics remain difficult to divine – the gardaí assumed that he was an IRA supporter because he had represented members on minor charges, but this assumption is not backed by any evidence, and his family had links to Cumann na nGaedheal. In 1948, Timoney became a TD for Clann na Poblachta, the republican party MacBride founded in 1946.

At the remand hearing on 19 December, MacBride appeared for the first time in this case, opposing any further remand. Judge Troy did grant a remand until 2 January 1941, but said that, after that, there would be no further remand.

So Harry Gleeson spent Christmas 1940 in Limerick Jail. For a while, he shared a cell with two (unrelated) prisoners called Ryan. The gardaí in New Inn told local people that Gleeson had confessed to his cellmates that he had murdered Moll McCarthy. Timoney got wind of this and went to the prison to demand that his client be moved to another cell, but Gleeson and the Ryans had already been separated. The alleged confession was never mentioned in the prosecution case but individual gardaí, including Frank Gralton, continued to speak of it as fact long after Gleeson was hanged.

While Harry Gleeson was locked up in prison in Limerick, and the younger McCarthy children were in care, Seán MacBride must have given some thought to the case he had taken on. It was, according to his recent biographer Caoimhe Nic Dháibhéid, the only non-republican capital case he took at that stage of his career. When MacBride looked down through the list of potential witnesses Timoney had begun to assemble, he saw names of people he knew through his own close involvement in the IRA for more than two decades, and others of whom he was aware because of their prominence in republican activities.

They included Jack 'The Boss' Nagle, who lived across the road from Moll, and who had not been at the 'gamble' at Lenehan's house on the night she went missing. He had been vice-commandant of the 6th Battalion of the Third Brigade of the IRA in south Tipperary; Thomas Hennessy, the witness who said he heard two shots coming from the direction of the Caesar farm at around 6 p.m. on Wednesday, 20 November, had also been a senior IRA commander. The intermarried O'Gorman and Byrne families, whose holdings adjoined John Caesar's, also had IRA connections, and were mentioned in Gleeson's statements to police. MacBride must also have known that Father Edward Murphy, who as parish priest of New Inn had earlier failed to get Moll's children taken away from her on the grounds of neglect, was also a senior IRA figure, who had been very active more than two decades earlier when MacBride joined the IRA. South Tipperary Fianna Fáil TD Frank Loughman had close connections with Father Murphy and Jack Nagle, and MacBride always liked to keep open a line of communication to those of republican inclination.

In 1940, MacBride stood at an intersection between politics and physical-force republicanism. Republicans respected him because he had been 'on active service', but were suspicious of his political leanings. Politicians respected him for his intellect and feared him for his republican pedigree and populist appeal. Though he was not long qualified as a barrister, his legal colleagues resented his forensic brilliance. He stood between law and illegality, carving out a meteoric career as a lawyer, yet playing the legal system in defence of gross illegality.

In Harry Gleeson's case, all these factors, plus local complications – like the shame of menfolk who had fathered children by Moll McCarthy, and the anger of their wives, sisters and mothers – came together in a web of great complexity, with MacBride close to the centre.

For complexity and causing paranoia among IRA supporters, nothing quite matched the case of the missing IRA man Michael Devereux. The garda manhunt for him, which began a few months before Moll McCarthy was murdered, was putting IRA sympathisers in south Tipperary under serious pressure. Sergeant Anthony Daly's recent transfer to New Inn from nearby Ballingarry was part of a strategy to turn up the heat on former IRA members by bringing in outsiders to shatter cosy relationships between police and the public in sensitive rural areas.

Michael Devereux, an IRA quartermaster in County Wexford, was missing, abducted by his comrades who thought he had informed to the police. Gardaí were hunting for Devereux and the people who abducted him in and around south Tipperary, where the IRA was known to have many sympathisers and safe houses. By the time Moll was murdered, Devereux was dead, but this was not public knowledge. George Plant, who led the IRA team that abducted Devereux, telling him they were protecting him, had moved him from a safe house in Grangemockler, County Tipperary. On 27 September 1940, Devereux thought he was being taken to another safe house, but on Gortnapisha Hill, Plant accused Devereux of being an informer and shot him in the head. In December 1940, Plant was arrested while cycling near Enniscorthy, County Wexford, and charged with IRA membership. In time he would face a firing squad for this murder. Devereux's body had not been found.

It is fair to assume that by then MacBride knew what the public did not know and what the gardaí suspected – that Devereux was dead. His IRA contacts would have told him. MacBride must have been aware of the likely network of safe houses, because Devereux was reputed to have been moved across the county, and wondered what this meant. Were the authorities closing in on the place where Devereux's body was buried? Or did they think he was still alive and could find him by raiding known IRA safe houses?

Gleeson was still in prison awaiting trial. While Moll McCarthy's murder had no direct connection with Devereux's fate, the hue and cry to find him was putting heat on known IRA supporters, people such as Nagle, Hennessy and the O'Gormans. Ardnassa, the home of the O'Gormans, adjoining Caesar's farm, was known to be an IRA safe house, as was the nearby Byrne house. Both had secret arms dumps on their land.[7] For them, the sooner the Moll McCarthy murder was dealt with, the better. At one stage, Devereux was thought to have been held in a safe house in Rosegreen, five miles by road, much less as the crow flies, from Marlhill. Sergeant Daly's known interest in what IRA sympathisers around New Inn were up to increased that tension.

On 2 January 1941, a preliminary hearing of the case against Harry Gleeson began in Clonmel. This was to establish if there was enough evidence to send him forward for a full trial at the Central Criminal Court in Dublin. Again, District Justice Troy was in charge, with George Murnaghan for the prosecution and Seán MacBride for the defence – both would continue their roles at the full trial. This preliminary hearing was held over three weeks. The full trial was completed within two weeks in February.

Much of the salient evidence will be dealt in the account of the Dublin trial in chapter three but some points occur. MacBride wished to inspect the daybook in New Inn garda station. The prosecution suspected that he wanted it to support Tommy Reid's case for assault in the station. It is not clear that Reid then knew that Chief Superintendent Reynolds was his main assailant; hence the need to identify who was present in the station on Monday, 25 November. Judge Troy refused to order that the daybook be handed over but suggested that MacBride had made a reasonable request and surely some compromise could be found. Murnaghan stiffly agreed to consider it, but MacBride never got what he was looking for.

MacBride kept a full note on the evidence given, and his impressions of witnesses. Twelve-year-old

Michael McCarthy gave evidence that he had seen his mother going out after teatime on Wednesday, 20 November.[8] In this court appearance he said he had not been at school that day, but had spent it playing around the yard behind the cottage. However, according to the school roll, Michael was at school that day. His oldest sister Mary clearly stated that Michael had been in school on the Wednesday. 'I remember Michael and Nellie coming home from school.' MacBride must have known that Michael's account of that day was suspect because he tried to subpoena the school attendance book for the main trial. The fact that he did not get it, and that neither of the teachers at the school came to the trial in Dublin to give evidence, as the defence wished,[9] may be because the school manager was also the parish priest. Father O'Malley's reluctance to do anything to help Harry Gleeson's defence was becoming increasingly noticeable. Gleeson was duly sent forward for trial in Dublin.

Among their problems, Moll McCarthy and her children had one they shared with John Caesar, and his nephew Harry Gleeson suffered from it too. They were 'blow-ins' and when trouble came to their doors, many local people, including those in positions of influence, turned their backs on them. Harry Gleeson, with whom Moll McCarthy's name would be for ever linked, was unmarried, about thirty-eight years old and had come to New Inn to manage his uncle's farm, a good farm which some local people would have preferred to remain in local hands.[10]

He had been born in 1903 near Holycross, some twenty miles from New Inn. One of twelve children of

Thomas Gleeson and Catherine Caesar, Harry grew up to be a good hurler, and was much in demand as a fiddle player, despite his occasional bouts of deafness. He had learned to read music from Dick Cantwell, a local virtuoso who gave music lessons in Cashel. Around 1920, his mother's brother, his Uncle John, offered him work on a farm at Graigue, New Inn, and a few years later, both men moved to a seventy-acre farm at nearby Marlhill. Over time, Harry's uncle handed over the management of the farm to him, in preparation for the day when the farm would be his, because John Caesar had no children from either marriage. In 1940 John Caesar was in his sixties and Bridget, his second wife, was probably about forty-five, according to Superintendent O'Mahony.

Even though Moll's mother had lived in her cottage before the Caesars arrived, none of the McCarthys ever really belonged to the community. A look at the roll book for Knockgraffon National School for 1871, the year it opened, shows that some family names – Hennessy, Nagle, Carew, Fitzgerald, Heffernan, English – are all present in the neighbourhood seventy years later when Moll was murdered.

Being outsiders in a tight-knit community, as both Harry Gleeson and Moll McCarthy were, also meant being excluded by an invisible wall of blood relationships and intermarriage. Moll McCarthy's cottage was surrounded on three sides by John Caesar's farm. Nearby, the O'Gorman and Byrne families were neighbours and had intermarried. Their holdings formed the southern boundary of John Caesar's farm. The field immediately south of the dug-out field, from which Harry Gleeson saw Moll's body lying, was known as Gorman's field. To the west lay Patrick Byrne's fields. Moll McCarthy's cottage was just up the road, past blacksmith Seanie Ryan's forge, and Jack Nagle lived a little farther up the road on the opposite side to Moll, but not as far away as the Fitzgeralds.

Jack Nagle's wife was Bird Fitzgerald. The Byrne family farm adjoined that of John Caesar, close to the O'Gorman house at Ardnassa. Patrick Byrne's wife Margaret was an O'Gorman. Before she married him in 1932, her husband had fathered Patrick McCarthy, Moll's second child, who was born around 1925. In 1927, Patrick Byrne of Knockgraffon was refused a pension for his IRA service but he seems to have got that later. He also had a pension for his service in the national army.

Separately from his work for John Caesar, Harry Gleeson and an agricultural contractor worked together during the harvest season, operating a threshing machine, which he hired out to farmers. John Caesar owned a binder, which Gleeson operated, and they charged a fee for their services. Some local people resented this commercialisation of the harvesting process because, traditionally, farmers helped each other out free of charge at harvest-time. However, it is hard to see how an expensive item like a threshing machine could have been financed without payment for its use.

There is also anecdotal evidence to show that Gleeson's deafness might have caused people to think that he was ignoring them when, in truth, he simply had not heard what they had said.

Almost every family in the immediate neighbour-hood of New Inn had an interest in the case of the murder of Moll McCarthy being dealt with as quickly as possible. Men who had used her for sex, women who knew or suspected that their sons or husbands had been involved with her, and their extended families, none would be in any hurry to come forward and so become implicated. The sooner this sorry affair was resolved, the better for everyone.

After Judge Seán Troy sent Harry for trial on a charge of murder, disturbing news interrupted Seán MacBride's preparations. Michael Devereux's wife Mary broadcast an appeal on Radio Éireann on 10 February 1941 for information on the whereabouts of her missing husband. This signalled to those in the know that the gardaí had a plan of some kind. It was impossible that the gardaí thought Devereux was still alive; some informer must have tipped them off. But what was their game? Nobody did paranoia like the IRA in the 1940s, and nobody was better at stoking it than the Garda Síochána Special Branch. Seven days later the trial of Henry Gleeson for the murder of Mary McCarthy began in Dublin.

# 3. Trial and Sentence

A s the case of the State versus Henry Gleeson began in Dublin, the first Royal Air Force flight via Irish airspace through the 'Donegal Corridor' between Northern Ireland and the Atlantic Ocean was about to take place, a concession secretly agreed by Taoiseach Éamon de Valera. Rommel's Afrika Korps was arriving in Tripoli, and Churchill was pleading with the United States to 'give us the tools and we'll finish the job' of defeating Germany and its allies.

The prosecution of Henry Gleeson for the murder of Mary McCarthy opened at the Central Criminal Court, sitting in Dublin's Green Street, close by the city's fruit-and-vegetable market. Judge Martin Maguire presided.[1] Joseph A. McCarthy SC, and George Murnaghan BL appeared for the prosecution; for the defence were James Nolan-Whelan SC and Seán MacBride BL. Jurors were chosen from the list of male domestic ratepayers; women at that time were excluded. Since working-class people rented rather than owned their houses, and thus did not directly pay rates, the jury was comprised of members of the Dublin middle class, and the legal teams were middle class, too. The defence and witnesses tended to have vocabularies and pastimes unfamiliar to Dubliners. Hare-coursing, for example, and frequenting shebeens (unlicensed drinking dens) were foreign pursuits to the prosperous Dublin merchant and professional classes. And in the formal language of court procedure 'Moll McCarthy' has become Mary McCarthy.

Unusually for an account of a criminal trial, we have a list of the names of the jurors, as follows:

Michael Campbell, foreman, restaurant proprietor, 90 Talbot Street.
Christopher Lambe, contractor, 15 Newgrove Avenue, Sandymount.
Louis Sandross, clerk, 147 Clonliffe Road, Drumcondra.
Joseph Fahy, draper's assistant, 55 Connaught Street, Phibsboro, jury foreman.
Joseph Halliday, accountant, 3 Belmont Grove, Donnybrook.
Henry Ivers, engineer, 271 Harold's Cross Road, Terenure.
Thomas Verling, grocer, 9 Conquer Hill Road, Glasnevin.
Joseph Parker, clerk, 109 South Circular Road, Kilmainham.
George Sargeant, insurance official, 13 Swords Road, Whitehall.
Andrew Wall, taxi owner, 18 Upper St Columba's Road, Glasnevin.

Andrew Thompson, auctioneer, 44 George's
Street, Dún Laoghaire.
Thomas Markey, clerk, 6 Temple Hill, Blackrock,
County Dublin.

When Gleeson was asked if he pleaded guilty or not
guilty, he replied: 'I had neither hand, act nor part in
the murder of Mary McCarthy.'

Two significant matters came up on the opening
day of the trial. The prosecution sought to change
the date on the indictment. Now Gleeson was
charged with murdering Mary McCarthy on or about
Wednesday 20 or Thursday 21 day of November
1940. He had previously been indicted on a charge
of murder simply on Thursday 21 November. The
defence reluctantly acceded to this change. 'I consent
to this amendment in order that all the facts relative
to the matter may be investigated,' Nolan-Whelan
said. As an experienced senior counsel, he should not
have let this one get past him.[2]

The question of when Mary McCarthy was
murdered remains a central mystery of the case to this
day. How long the body was lying in the field – or
elsewhere before being taken to the field – has never
been satisfactorily answered. Was she murdered
on the evening of Wednesday 20 November? Or
on the following morning? Was she murdered in
the field on John Caesar's farm where the body was
found? Or perhaps in a nearby disused farmhouse?
Or somewhere else? These questions were never
satisfactorily resolved in court.

Nolan-Whelan applied to have the prosecution's
opening address to the jury taken down by the official

stenographer. He feared that prosecuting counsel, Joseph A. McCarthy, would 'over-egg the pudding', and prejudice Gleeson's chance of a fair trial. But Judge Maguire would have none of it, and the stage was set for a very tetchy ten-day trial, eight days of which would pass before Gleeson's side of the argument was put to the jury.

McCarthy began to outline the prosecution's case. Although the court stenographer did not record his words, the *Clonmel Nationalist* did, and McCarthy began by saying that on the morning of Thursday, 21 November, the accused, Gleeson, knocked on the door of New Inn garda station and reported: 'There is a woman dead in the back of the ditch in Caesar's field near the dug-out.' This, said McCarthy, '... was the first intimation the garda authorities got of a murder that was as crafty, as cold-blooded as the mind of man could conceive – a murder that had a sordid and squalid background.'

When the station sergeant Anthony Daly asked Gleeson what had happened, he replied that he had been out counting sheep when he saw the body. 'I got up on the ditch to count them. She appeared to be dead. There was a dog with her and for that reason I did not go near her. I went back to Caesar's house and told them about what I had seen and came here through the fields to report.'

As the gardaí made their way to the scene, they asked Gleeson if he knew who the victim was. 'He replied he did not go near her. He did not know her, she might only be asleep.'

Joseph McCarthy declared that this was just one of the many steps Gleeson took to conceal his own

Dug-out field

The view from the dug-out field into the stubble field where the body was lying behind the tree or large bush on the left. Gleeson said he stood in the gap looking into the field. COURTESY FIONA ARYAN

associations with the murder, to divert attention from his own responsibility, to convey to the gardaí his willingness to assist and to put himself forward as a person whose conduct was consistent with innocence and the desire to assist justice. Of course, there was the possibility that Gleeson was telling the truth – but McCarthy's job was to secure a conviction of the man in the dock, and so he painted a picture of a manipulative man.

McCarthy continued to brief the jury, saying that when the gardaí approached where the body was lying, at a distance – put by one garda at six yards and by another at eight yards – they easily recognised the body as that of Mary McCarthy, a neighbour of the accused.

> She was a gruesome sight. She had been shot like a wild beast. One shot had been fired into her at a range of five or six feet, fired at a time when at least the upper portion of the body was erect: fired from the left, entering her neck. The gunshot made a hole about three-quarters of an inch in diameter, severing an artery, the jugular vein and fracturing the spine. When she fell and was lying on the ground, either dead or in the last throes of her death agony, the same gun was placed in close proximity to her face, and the face was blown away.

Here, even McCarthy's florid language is not equal to the horrors of the scene he describes. Garda photographs of Moll McCarthy's corpse, taken on the day her body was discovered, show that very little of her face had survived the shots. A body with the face blown away is a truly ghastly sight, as the jury discovered. But McCarthy had a further point to make: that Gleeson was a liar as well as a murderer. Noting that some of the victim's teeth and bones had been driven into the ground, he continued: 'That was the woman whom the accused said is dead or may be sleeping.'[3]

The prosecution would show that the murder was committed by design and by deliberation and by some person who knew Moll and her plans, by somebody whose presence on Caesar's land would not be a surprise and who had easy access to that land and a means of escape.

McCarthy also claimed that the mutilation of the body was an attempt to conceal the victim's identity, but it is doubtful if he actually believed that, or expected anyone else to.

The first major building block in the case against Gleeson had been put in place. He had seen Moll McCarthy lying dead in the field and had pretended not to recognise her.

Joseph A. McCarthy then set out the rest of the case against Gleeson in broad outline. First, he described the set-up on the Caesar farm. The household consisted of John and Bridget Caesar, John's nephew Harry, and a workman named Tommy Reid. Gleeson managed the farm for his uncle and expected to inherit it, because the Caesars were elderly and had no children. John Caesar had a single-barrelled shotgun and kept it in the farm kitchen[4] with its cleaning rod and ammunition, which both he and Gleeson – among others – used for scaring off crows and for shooting vermin.

On 3 October 1940, about six weeks before the murder, John Caesar bought twenty-five Eley brand cartridges in Feehan's hardware shop in Cashel.

This is the second building block in the case against Gleeson: Moll was shot with a single-barrelled shotgun. This 'fact' formed a bedrock part of the prosecution case and yet it is entirely possible and even likely that she was shot with a double-barrelled shotgun – neither counsel nor the judge appear to have understood the difference.

McCarthy's initial presentation of the prosecution case was that the murder victim had lived in a humble cottage on a little plot of ground surrounded on three sides by John Caesar's farm. She was the unfortunate mother of seven illegitimate children, six of whom, three girls and three boys, were living with her, She was entitled to free milk and got potatoes from Gleeson. Gleeson gave her the potatoes without his uncle's approval, since any connection with her could prevent him inheriting the farm that he felt was his. McCarthy told the jury that Mary McCarthy paid Gleeson for the potatoes with sex.

'What was the association between Gleeson and Mary McCarthy?' Joseph A. McCarthy had asked before answering his own question.

He told the jury that, from the evidence of the 'association', they would see that it could properly be described as an immoral relationship. Mary McCarthy met Gleeson at the pump where she and her family went for water. Prosecution counsel is here referring to the field pump, though he did not make that clear. Sometimes when she went to that pump and Gleeson was there, she sent away any of her children who had accompanied her. She would be seen going away from the pump with Gleeson and would not return to her cottage for some time. Gleeson was also seen at the pump, signalling to Mary McCarthy to come to him across the fields, and he had also been seen signalling to her from a point sixty yards from her home.

Dealing with the events of Wednesday, 20 November – the last full day of Moll McCarthy's life – McCarthy told the jury that she had left home at about 5.30 p.m. and had met Gleeson soon after.

Gleeson had then killed Moll with two shots, heard by a neighbour, Thomas Hennessy.

In essence, the prosecution case outlined by Joseph A. McCarthy relied on circumstantial evidence to show that Gleeson had an affair with Moll and that she had become demanding. Counsel claimed that, to stop Moll telling the Caesars about his immoral relationship with her, which would lead to him being disinherited, Gleeson had killed her. He had then left her mutilated body in a field overnight before 'discovering' it the following morning and reporting it to the police, claiming that he did not recognise whose body it was. It is worth noting that the prosecution has already narrowed the case against Harry Gleeson to one day, the Wednesday evening, having just amended the charge to either Wednesday or Thursday.

The first witness was then called. Garda William Quinlan of the technical unit at garda headquarters in Dublin gave evidence of the measurements taken at the scene where the body was found. He had used these measurements to produce a map of the scene.

The first thing to be said is that Quinlan made a serious mistake in the placing of the body on the map. Instead of the body lying close to the hedge or ditch, with the feet pointing in Gleeson's direction, and the little dog on the woman's chest, it was now much farther out in the field – in full view for all to see. The effect of this was to render incredible Gleeson's assertion that he had not recognised the body. The defence naturally sought to maximise the opportunity this mistake offered.

The judge corrected the error, telling the jury that the map placed the body in the wrong part of the field.

The jury should remember the photographs given in evidence, the judge said, which showed the body had lain in a more secluded place in the corner of the field than Quinlan's map indicated.

Further argument was procedural and difficult to follow as Garda Quinlan used a colour coding which is not easy to follow at this remove. Another difficulty is that the contours of the land appear misleadingly flat. Much evidence rested on who could see what and from where. How much of the body could Gleeson be expected to see over the ditch separating two fields on quite different levels? The same question would arise later – how much of Caesar's farm could Moll's children see from their cottage? Michael McCarthy would later claim to have seen Gleeson in the stubble field on the Thursday morning; the defence would contend that this was not possible from where the boy said he was standing.

Quinlan's evidence continued into the second day of the trial and led to a serious and personalised conflict between the judge who was, it seems clear, overly protective of Garda Quinlan, and the defence which continued to make out that the fault in the map was a deliberate attempt to subvert Gleeson's plea of innocence.

As the first day's hearing finished, Nolan-Whelan, Gleeson's senior counsel, asked the judge to order the prosecution to give the defence copies of a 'statement made by Michael McCarthy and the other child' (his older brother, Patrick) which the chief state solicitor's office had refused to provide.

The judge replied that 'when the court is adjourned, it is not the moment to make the application' but he offered little hope that a more timely application would be granted. This, too, would prove to be a further item of contention between the defence and the prosecution.

Nolan-Whelan was right to push this point, because the 'statement' by the McCarthy sons, which took the form of notes compiled by Superintendent O'Mahony, proved to be very damaging to Gleeson. If Nolan-Whelan had got sight of this document before Michael and Patrick McCarthy gave evidence, and had been able to question them about it, the trial might have come to an early end with the discharge of the accused.

**DAY TWO**

*Tuesday, 18 February 1941*

On the second day of the trial, twelve-year-old Michael McCarthy was the main witness. Moll's second son proved to be an unsatisfactory witness and he could not have been anything else. His already difficult young life had been shattered by the brutal murder of his mother less than three months earlier. Giving evidence in a murder trial is stressful, and the arcane practices of the court at the time made fewer concessions to a child witness than is the case today. There were hidden hazards. Even words like 'dinner', 'supper' and 'tea' had different meanings in a cottage in County Tipperary than they had in the leafy suburbs of Dublin. And Michael, whose school attendance record was poor, lacked the vocabulary to understand fully and answer the questions he was asked. His stint in the witness box took up most of the second day, and during that time 500 questions were put to him. Some he found difficult to answer; others impossible. Many simply went unanswered despite encouragement from judge and counsel.

The first few questions that prosecution counsel George Murnaghan asked Michael McCarthy were innocuous enough, about how many brothers and sisters he had, and about going to school. He continued.

'Now, Michael, do you remember the day your mammy went away and did not come back again?'

'Yes, sir.'

'She went away after her tea and did not come back again. On that day, were you at school?'

'Yes, sir.'

'Did you come home from school?'

'Yes.'

'Who was home along with you?

'My sister Ellen [also known as Nellie].'

'What time did you come home?'

'About three o'clock.'

Nothing unusual there, just the second prosecution lawyer, in his low-key way, establishing the whereabouts of a young witness, as an important part of the trial got under way. Except this: Michael has changed his story. At the committal hearing before Judge Seán Troy barely a month earlier, Michael had said that he was *not* at school on Wednesday, the day his mother went missing. 'I spent it around the yard,' he said when asked what he had done instead of going to school.[5]

Murnaghan continued to ask Michael leading questions, until finally Nolan-Whelan objected. For example:

'What happened after the meal? What did you do yourself?'

'I went down to change the spancel on the ass [the tether on the donkey].'

'Was that down the field?'

'Yes, sir.'

'After you had changed the spancel on the ass, what did you do?'

'I came up to the house, sir, and played around the yard.'

'When you were playing around the yard, did you see your mother?'

'Yes, sir.'

This could not continue. Murnaghan was 'leading the witness' – in effect giving the child's evidence for him. Nolan-Whelan objected but the judge told him he had no grounds thus far to object. Nolan-Whelan countered that the child's memory of the events described needed to be tested. The judge agreed with this and warned Murnaghan that the court had to hear the witness give evidence in his own words.

Judge Martin Maguire also often intervened to question young Michael directly. He had been recently appointed to the bench, and his frequent 'taking over' of the prosecution case, questioning witnesses from the bench, soon became a marked feature of the trial.

After the McCarthy family had eaten together – all except Patrick – Michael said that he had seen his mother go out across the fields. Michael had gone to Condon's house nearby and been paid for the servicing of a female goat, which had taken place earlier that day. (Michael came to her house after

6 p.m. according to Mrs Condon's later testimony.) When he got home, his brother Patrick had arrived. Patrick visited his mother and brothers and sisters most days, Michael said, although he slept at Hanley's farm where he worked.

Michael said that when he went to bed, his mother had not come home. Because of this, Patrick had stayed overnight in the cottage, but he got up and went to work the following morning. After lighting the fire and eating breakfast, Michael went out 'down the fields', he said.

Where he was going is hard to tell. He was not on his way to school, which lay in the opposite direction. The land generally slopes south to north, and he described going along the 'horse field' a little over halfway between the McCarthy cottage and the laneway leading to Caesar's farm.

The judge intervened. 'Did you see anything as you were going up along that field?'

'Yes, sir. I saw Harry jump from the dug-out field to the stubble field.'

In other words, Gleeson had been in the two fields at the very centre of the case before he said he was. Also, Michael had seen him jumping over the ditch *and* into the stubble field where Moll's body would be found.

This assertion – in advance of his own account – makes a liar of Gleeson. At the time Michael McCarthy claimed to have seen him, Gleeson had told gardaí that he was out and about checking on his uncle's fields and looking for the bull and sheep. Gleeson maintained that he did not enter the stubble field where Moll's body was lying, saying he only jumped up on the ditch to look for the sheep, saw the body lying near the side of the field with the small dog crouched on top of it. The dog lying on the body growled and, because Gleeson had Vincent Scully's greyhound[6] with him, he went no farther; instead he ran back to Caesar's house to raise the alarm.

There was no evidence, apart from Michael's sighting across two or three fields, that Gleeson had entered the stubble field at that time.

It is remarkable that, at this point, the judge could not contain himself. It seems that this strand of the case against Gleeson was so important to the judge that it could not be left to the prosecution counsel to deal with. Maguire took over the questioning, asking where Michael was, how he got there, and if he had been running.

Murnaghan eventually did manage to retrieve the examination of Michael McCarthy, asking him if the man he saw in the stubble field with a greyhound was in court. Michael positively identified Gleeson. 'The greyhound was running around loose in the field,' the boy said. According to Gleeson, the greyhound was on a leash, and never crossed the ditch between the dug-out field and the stubble field.

Michael had given evidence about seeing his mother and Gleeson arguing earlier in the day. He also said that he had heard his mother tell Gleeson that 'she would put him up to the law to pay for the last child' – the baby Peggy who had been born the previous May but who had died soon afterwards. That row, for which we have only Michael's word, took place a month after the baby had died. Michael was saying that Gleeson was the father of that child, though no proof of this was put before the court or has arisen since. We can be reasonably certain that Gleeson did not father any of Moll's seven children.

Michael also said that sometimes – though he could not say how often – he went with his mother to the well in Caesar's field, usually used for watering cattle. This well was in the pump field, not the one near to the Caesar farmhouse. He said that Gleeson and his mother would talk at the well and that his mother would tell Michael to go home and that she would follow later.

Michael could not recall drawing water with his mother from the pump in Caesar's field after his half-sister Peggy was born. Under cross-examination by Nolan-Whelan, Michael said that he often heard Gleeson complaining to his mother about the trespassing goats, but he could not recall when or where these complaints had been made. Sometimes Gleeson chased the goats off the land, sometimes Moll did and sometimes he – Michael – did. On occasion, the goats went into the boggy field called the Moonthawn, close to Caesar's field pump, and Gleeson and Moll had gone there after them. Later, Michael said that after Peggy's death the family had obtained water from Halpin's pump. This can be partially explained by evidence given elsewhere that in summer the field pump water tended to have a brackish taste and was well nigh undrinkable. (We now have four sources of water in this case – one in Caesar's pump field, closest to the McCarthy cottage, one in Caesar's yard, one belonging to Halpin, and Landy's pump, of which no further detail was given, except that it did not provide water all year round. Michael also mentioned in evidence Leamy's pump, but this appears to be Landy's pump, with the name garbled. It is no wonder the child and the jury became confused. Marcus Bourke, author of *Murder at Marlhill*, concluded that Michael McCarthy was lying at this stage.)

Michael testified that his family used to get potatoes from their neighbours, the Halpins, and also sometimes from Gleeson. One night, his mother sent him and his brother Patrick to the bottom of the black ditch[7] where they found a 'butt of spuds' on the ground. He said that, after his mother's death, he saw bags taken by the gardaí from John Caesar's yard. One of those bags belonged to his mother. He had last seen it in their own shed the Sunday before his mother died. The prosecution would say that the bag ended up in the Caesar's house because Moll had given the bag to Gleeson to fill with potatoes to bring to her, so she would provide sex in return.

Michael also gave evidence about callers to their home. His mother used to have visitors, some in the daytime, some in the evening. Tinkers and tramps also came to the McCarthy house. In an exchange between the judge and prosecution counsel Murnaghan, the judge noted that the boy was in effect giving evidence that his mother was keeping an 'open house' for men looking for sex, though both men agreed that the boy could not be expected to realise the implications of what he was saying. Michael also gave evidence that Sergeant Daly had called to the house in the afternoon a few hours before his mother had gone out for the last time. No explanation was sought or given for that visit.

Michael described his mother wearing a costume of grey and black stripes the last time he had seen her when she was leaving the cottage to go across the fields. This conflicts with the state pathologist's deposition describing what Moll was wearing when he examined her body. What also went unchallenged was Michael's statement to the court that he was at school on the Wednesday, having sworn to the contrary the previous month. The prosecution examination of Michael McCarthy was allowed to continue as if nothing untoward had happened. We can only conclude that neither MacBride nor his senior Nolan-Whelan spotted that Michael had changed his story. Jurors might have been liable to dismiss minor discrepancies in a child's evidence but would no doubt have been worried by one that would have cast doubt on his recollection of the sequence of events.[8]

Michael's evidence could well have been about the 'wrong' day. He also said it took him about an hour to get to school, whereas twenty minutes would suffice. This also put his evidence about days and time in doubt. Nolan-Whelan should have seen this from looking at the maps that had been provided and comparing witness statements. Under questioning, Michael had admitted that he could not read the time from a clock, nor count beyond ten. Neither did he know the age of his youngest brother, Connie.

Michael McCarthy had begun giving evidence in the morning and his questioning continued for much of the afternoon. When his older brother Patrick followed him into the witness box, there was a noticeable change in tone. Patrick's evidence is more measured, perhaps reflecting the three-year age difference, but also, I believe, his account had not been coached to the same extent as Michael's.

Patrick said that when he called to his home after work at about 7 p.m. on the evening of Wednesday, 20 November, his mother was missing. At around 11 p.m., he went around Caesar's farm with a dog to look for her. The following day, when he was shown where the body had lain, he realised that he had been in the stubble field the previous night but had not seen his mother. Given that Harry Gleeson had ploughed much of that field earlier that day, Patrick would have had to stay close to the hedge, and he, or his dog, would surely have seen his mother if she had been lying in the spot she was found. He said he had remained there, listening for sounds, for about five minutes, because he was anxious about his mother. He had not gone back to Hanley's farm where he worked but had stayed in the family cottage, going to bed at about 1 a.m.

Under questioning from the prosecution, Patrick said he had known Gleeson as long as he could remember. He saw him 'keeping company' with his mother, the phrase suggesting an intimate relationship, but it was not clear that he meant it in that way. The context for their short encounters – usually when Gleeson was complaining to her about her trespassing goats, or exchanging gossip – suggests that they often were in each other's presence, but not in a planned way. According to Patrick, they used to be down in the corner of one field, Gleeson on his side of the ditch, his mother on hers.

The eldest of Moll's children – Mary McCarthy, aged nineteen – was the final witness of the trial's second day. She recalled Michael and her sister Nellie returning from school on the Wednesday. She also said she had frequently seen her mother talking to Gleeson. About a month before her mother died, Mary had seen her talking in a friendly way to Gleeson. She said it had just been getting dark when her mother went out for the last time on Wednesday, 20 November, but she could not say the exact time.

Whatever opinion one may have about the veracity of Michael McCarthy's evidence, we can see that he did very well for a twelve-year-old and there is no doubt that he had been schooled by the gardaí in what to say. The lies about school attendance (at some stage Michael had lied, either to the committal hearing or to the murder trial) could be explained by the fact that his mother was frequently in trouble with the law about her children's poor attendance at school, and she had probably told them that if anyone asked them, they were to say they were in school, whether that was true or not. Elsewhere it was stated that Garda Joseph Ruth had called to the McCarthy cottage to discuss her children's non-attendance at school two days before Moll went missing.

But now, two days into the prosecution case, the jury had been told in so many words that Harry Gleeson and Moll were lovers and that her three eldest children understood that he was the father of her last child, and that she kept an open house for sex – the logic of the prosecution case went – so the murder would have followed from that.

But the jury did not know that Michael's evidence about his movements on Wednesday, 20 November was riddled with holes. It was smart of the prosecution to build so much of its case on the back of a twelve-year-old boy who had suffered such a great loss. His testimony was shaky at best, but the defence could not risk a hostile cross-examination. Giving a child a hard time in the witness box over the events surrounding the violent death of his mother was a very quick route to inflaming judge and jury against the defence.

For the prosecution, getting this evidence out of the way early in the trial meant that much of the 'heavy lifting' in the case was now done.

### DAY THREE

## Wednesday, 19 February 1941

The third morning's hearing began with a neighbour James Condon, giving evidence of passing the McCarthy cottage on the morning and evening of Wednesday, 20 November and seeing nothing unusual. During the afternoon he had taken a goat to McCarthy's to be serviced by the billy goat. He had not see Moll McCarthy then. Michael McCarthy had come to his house to be paid for the services of the billy goat at around 6 p.m., and to collect milk. He had stayed for half an hour while the cows were milked. Later, after midnight, Condon had passed the McCarthy cottage on his way home from Lenehan's 'gamble' and had seen a light in the kitchen.

He then went on to say that the next morning he saw Michael McCarthy standing on top of a heap of manure, looking in the direction of the Caesar farm. This partially confirms Michael's account of looking across the fields when he claimed he saw Gleeson jumping down off the ditch into the stubble field where Moll's body was stretched out. Condon said nothing about seeing Gleeson, however. Condon's wife Margaret took the stand and gave evidence of providing milk for the McCarthy family under the home assistance scheme. John Purcell, a home assistance officer, confirmed that the McCarthys got six shillings' worth of milk per week, supplied by the Condons.

Shortly afterwards, another neighbour, William O'Gorman, gave evidence. O'Gorman repeated to the court what he had said in his earlier deposition to gardaí: 'I live at Ardnassa, New Inn. I have lived there all my life. I knew the late Mary McCarthy of Marlhill. She was never in my house. She was never expected to call at my house. She had no business at or about my house on or about 20 November 1940.'

What is not clear is why O'Gorman went to such lengths to tell the court that Moll was never in his house. No one had asked him about whether or not she had visited him. He offered the information unprompted. Why? Was he trying to forestall any suspicion of his being implicated in Moll McCarthy's murder? Or of having had an improper association with her? Why did he ensure that his denial covered the date 'on or about' which the police had said the murder took place?

You would never guess from this that William O'Gorman's brother-in-law, Patrick Byrne, was the father of Moll's second child, Patrick, and that this was common knowledge around New Inn. Nor that William's brother Pak had an interest in the outcome of the trial.

Some other neighbours of John Caesar's briefly gave evidence. More substantial evidence followed before lunchtime when three gardaí from New Inn station appeared in the witness box. First Garda Vincent Scully described events of the morning of Thursday, 21 November when Gleeson arrived at the police station and reported seeing an unknown woman lying in a field on Caesar's farm. According to Scully, Gleeson said: 'When I came to the corner of a field near the dug-out, I looked over the ditch into the ploughed field, and saw the woman and she appeared to be dead. There was a small black dog with her. I heard the dog whimper and for that reason I did not go near her. I went back to Caesars' and told them what I'd seen. I came here to report it.' Sergeant Daly, who had been summoned from his living quarters upstairs in the barracks, then left the room and Scully asked Gleeson how he knew that the body was that of a woman. He replied: 'I knew by the petticoat and shoes.'[9]

Garda Scully told James Nolan-Whelan that he did not remember details of a conversation between Garda Ruth and Gleeson in the garda station. Scully said that Gleeson's hearing was slightly defective, but not bad. 'Gleeson appeared normal.'

Then Garda Frank Gralton confirmed Scully's account of the conversation in the garda station. He remembered looking at Gleeson's watch, which showed 9.30 a.m. old time. Gralton's own watch showed 10.22 a.m. new time, or a difference of about eight minutes when the mismatch between 'old' and 'new' time is factored in. Gleeson had been in the station for less than five minutes, he thought.

This meant that it took Gleeson thirty to forty minutes from the first sighting of the body in the field to get to the police station. Even allowing for the fact that he went back to the Caesars' yard and secured Scully's greyhound and the farm dogs, and that he had to locate the Caesars and tell them what had happened, it should have taken him about fifteen minutes by the shortcut, or Mass path, across the field to the back of the garda station.

Garda Joseph Ruth, who followed Gralton into the witness box, said that he, Sergeant Anthony Daly and Gleeson then went by garda car to Caesar's farm. Approaching the stubble field from the west, Ruth said he had no difficulty in identifying the body as Moll McCarthy from a distance of about eight yards. He said to Sergeant Daly, 'It is Mary McCarthy all right.'

According to the evidence given in court, this was the first time Mary McCarthy's name was mentioned in connection with the body in the field. Bill O'Connor in his account[10] makes much of this; for him it is an admission that Moll was already known to be the victim. Under cross-examination, Garda Ruth denied this meaning and said Seán MacBride was reading too much into it.

However, there is also the possibility that the formal taking of statements has polluted the record of what was said. In speech Garda Ruth probably would have called her Moll McCarthy, not least to distinguish her from her daughter Mary. The 'all right' could even be a rhetorical flourish added at the barracks room table. What was not contested in court is Gleeson's assertion that initially he had not recognised that it was Moll McCarthy.

But this is hard to believe, and it is likely the jury thought so too.

The most likely scenario is that Gleeson ran back to the Caesars' home, told his uncle and his aunt what he had seen, and Mrs Caesar had urged him to go and tell the gardaí, but not to say any more than that, saying something like: 'Don't let on you know who it is. Just tell them to come.'

Bridget Caesar must have known that any admission of association with Moll could now be very dangerous for Harry Gleeson. How many mothers have said something similar to their sons, and Bridget Caesar was Harry's mother in all but name? But that simple deception could have cost him his life. There has to be some reason why Gleeson said he did not recognise the body. Years later, Caesar's farmhand Tommy Reid told Marcus Bourke that Gleeson *had* recognised Moll when he had seen her body, and he confirmed that Bridget Caesar had told Gleeson and himself to say nothing and keep their mouths shut.

Another reason to think that Gleeson must have recognised the body is that, if he had not, Bridget Caesar would have sent Tommy Reid to the field while Gleeson fetched the police. It would have been out of character for her not to find out what was wrong and to see if there was anything to be done. But in encouraging Gleeson not to tell the full story to the police, she cast doubt on his veracity on other matters, and deprived the defence of the opportunity to call her or her husband as character witnesses, lest they be asked what Gleeson had said to them on the morning he found the body. The truth could hang him, yet perjury was impossible.

Not telling people any more than you think they need to know is not an uncommon habit in rural Ireland. It is not confined to south Tipperary, and it persists to this day.

Soon after midday, Sergeant Anthony Daly gave evidence. When he had asked Gleeson what was wrong, he said that Gleeson had replied, 'When I was out counting sheep this morning, I got up on the ditch to count them in another field. There was a woman lying in the field. She appeared to be dead. There was a dog on the body.'

Daly had asked him if he recognised the person lying in the field. According to Daly, Gleeson replied, 'I did not know her. She was wearing a blue dress. She may not be dead.'

Note that the grey and black striped costume Michael described has now become a blue dress. Later on their way to where the body lay, Daly had asked Gleeson again if it was a local person. Gleeson repeated, 'I did not go near her. I did not know her.' When he was questioned further, he said he did not know whose dog was on the body.

When they arrived at the scene, Sergeant Daly and Garda Ruth approached the body. Daly told the court that he had recognised the body as that of Moll McCarthy when they were about six yards from it. He said he had seen her about five or six times. Daly said there was a small dog standing on the body eating the face. He removed the dog and told Gleeson to get a sheet with which to cover the body. Gleeson went and got one from the house. When that was done, Daly had walked to the Caesars' farmhouse with Gleeson in silence, and had then gone back to New Inn to report the murder to his superiors.

Court file photograph of John Caesar's house, since demolished.
COURTESY NATIONAL ARCHIVES

When Daly returned to the scene, he removed the sheet and found gunshot pellets on the left-hand side of the collar of the corpse's coat, two shotgun cartridge wads close together and three pieces of bone on the left-hand side of the face. Daly said he had remained at the scene until around 3 p.m., just under two hours after Dr O'Connor arrived.

In later cross-examination, the defence did not ask Sergeant Daly what business had brought him to Moll McCarthy's house at around 3.30 p.m. on the Wednesday, just hours before she disappeared. A garda source familiar with the case told me in 2012 that it could have been about summonses for non-attendance of her children at school.[11] Local sources in New Inn told Marcus Bourke that Daly had more personal business with her.[12]

According to the medical evidence given a couple of days later in court, Moll had consensual sexual intercourse not long before she died, but we simply cannot know if it was with Daly or with one of the men who might have been responsible for her death.

Most of the cross-examination of Sergeant Daly related to allegations of the maltreatment of Tommy Reid at New Inn garda station. However, Daly flatly rejected any suggestion that Tommy Reid had been beaten up during his more than twelve hours in the station. This was a direct lie.

John Halpin, a 65-year-old farmer, was next to give evidence. He said he lived up the road, to the north of Moll McCarthy's house and farmed sixteen acres adjoining John Caesar's land, including a small paddock near the Moonthawn, a boggy field, where Moll sometimes drew water from a pump (the field pump). Halpin's fields were essentially a chunk bitten out of John Caesar's farm from the north, just as Moll's cottage did on the south-west flank, but in a more modest way.

The defence objected to Halpin giving evidence of a conversation between himself and Gleeson over the birth of Moll's last child, but Judge Martin Maguire ruled that it was admissible evidence. Halpin said that Gleeson had asked him if he knew about the birth of Peggy, and Halpin said he did not.

Halpin spoke of going to the field pump to draw water for his own cattle, and suggesting to Gleeson that he stop Moll from using the field pump and to go back to drawing water from the pump in the Caesars' yard, given her 'pedigree'.

'Did you tell him why?' Joseph McCarthy asked Halpin.

'Yes, that he might avoid becoming associated with the scandal. If other people saw Mary McCarthy draw the pump water, they might not understand the position as well as I did.'

It is possible to see in this a suggestion that Halpin believed that Gleeson could have had an intimate relationship with Moll, and that Halpin was gently warning him to watch his step. But it could also have been a warning from the older man to Gleeson about the risk of provoking gossip, well founded or not.

Halpin also gave evidence of meeting Gleeson six days before Moll's body was found, 'carrying a bucket of milk in one hand and a gun in the other'. He had remarked on how clean the gun was. This had significance inasmuch as the prosecution would later claim that Gleeson used the gun frequently.

Halpin also told the court that Gleeson was a 'hard-working chap, very industrious about his uncle's affairs' and that, personally, he had always found Moll to be a 'very quiet, inoffensive woman'.

## DAY FOUR

### *Thursday, 20 February 1941*

The fourth day of the trial effectively began with Tommy Reid's evidence. He told the court that he was twenty-four years old and had lived and worked on John Caesar's farm for nine years. He remembered the day before Moll McCarthy's body was found because it had been fair day and the Caesars had gone to Cashel to sell pigs. He gave evidence of being with Gleeson for much of the day. Gleeson had come in from ploughing the stubble field at about 4.30 p.m. and had stabled the horses, while Reid ate his supper alone about 5.30 or 5.50 p.m. after milking the cows in the field where the pump was. Gleeson came in at about 6 p.m. In turn, Gleeson was eating his supper when Tommy left to visit a neighbour's house.

Reid specifically remembered Gleeson coming in a minute after the farmhouse clock had struck six, and that there was nothing unusual in his manner or appearance. He had never seen Gleeson giving Moll McCarthy potatoes and had never heard any suggestion that Gleeson was the father of her last child. Reid told the court that the shotgun was ordinarily kept in John Caesar's bedroom, except on the days when it was being used, in which case it was left beside the dresser in the kitchen.

Joseph A. McCarthy for the prosecution started the questioning.

> 'About the Thursday morning – who was up first?'
> 'Harry Gleeson.'
> 'Was it he called you?'
> 'Yes.'
> 'And what did ye do when you got up?'
> 'We got up and lit the fire, and got a cup of tea, then he went out to feed the horses; after that we had [another] cup of tea and we went over [the fields to do the] milking.'

The judge intervened. 'The two of you had tea together?'

'Yes.'

McCarthy continued. 'Who lit the fire? Was the fire lit before you went down?'

'Yes. Gleeson called me.'

The judge intervened again. 'You were asked was the fire lit, or did you light it?'

'The fire was lit.'

'Why did you say you lit the fire?' the judge asked.

'Well, he hadn't got it lit in full.'

McCarthy continued. 'Then you fed the horses and milked the cows?'

'Yes.'

'That is the usual morning's work?'

'Yes.'

'What time did you get back [to the house]?'

'It could be about nine o'clock or a quarter past.' [This was later clarified as being old time.]

'Was Gleeson with you when you got back?'

'Yes.'

The judge then asked, 'Was he milking with you?'

'Yes.'

Nolan-Whelan then cross-examined Reid for the defence and Reid told him that his timings were approximate.

'With reference to Mary McCarthy going to the pump at Caesar's house, had she been going there for water from the time nine years ago that you went to Caesar's?'

'Yes.'

'During all that period, on and off, she went to Caesar's house [meaning yard] pump?'
'Yes.'

The point that Nolan-Whelan is trying to get across is that the pump in Caesar's yard was a more public place than the pump in the field, where Gleeson and Moll were alleged to be 'keeping company'.

Later in the morning of the fourth day, there was a prolonged spat between Judge Martin Maguire and Tommy Reid over whether or not Tommy believed Gleeson when the older man told him he had not recognised Moll's little black dog. Tommy said he did believe him. The exchange was significant as evidence of Maguire's dislike of anyone whose evidence did not suit his view of the case.

Reid said Gleeson was a good-living, decent, sober fellow. Tommy Reid then said he was invited into New Inn garda station to make a statement at about 9.30 or 10 a.m. on Monday, 25 November and that he did not leave until around 11 p.m.[13] that evening. He said that while he was at the station, he was pressed to make a false statement about Gleeson, but he refused. He said that gardaí then beat him. The next morning, he went to the doctor because his face was bruised and to the parish priest, Father O'Malley, to show him the injuries to his face.

The judge asked Reid to be more specific about the false statements he was asked to make. In doing so, the judge again took on the role of prosecuting counsel to question Reid about what had happened in the barracks.

*Judge*: 'What were the false statements you were pressed to make by members of the civic guards?'

*Reid*: 'They [the two gardaí named Reynolds] wanted me to say that … yes that Gleeson was going back to bed that morning the body was found.'

*Judge*: 'What do you mean by that?'

*Reid*: 'That in place of getting up that morning he was going back to bed when he came in to call me to get up.' [The implication being that Gleeson had been out earlier and could have committed the murder then.]

*Judge*: 'Is that the only false statement you were asked to say?'

*Reid*: 'He wanted me to say yes, he was the father of the last child.'

*Judge*: 'That was a tall order, to ask you to say that Gleeson was the father of the last child. Were you astonished to be asked to say such a thing?'

*Reid*: 'Well I didn't see why I should be beat —'

*Judge* (*interrupts*): 'What else were you asked to say that was false?'

*Reid*: 'That it was Gleeson who buried the child.'

Reid told the judge that he had refused to do so, and was taking a case against the gardaí over his ill treatment. He had identified the gardaí responsible; Sergeant Daly was not one of them. Tommy Reid also said he had not known about the death of Moll's last child. Reid's evidence concluded with him confirming that gardaí had asked him to lie only on the three points above. The transcript of the court hearing does not indicate if the judge handed back the interrogation to prosecuting counsel Joseph McCarthy before Reid's evidence concluded.

At this point, it is worth standing back and looking at what was going on. Tommy Reid had given Gleeson an alibi for the two most likely occasions when he could have killed Moll, the Wednesday evening at around 6 p.m., and early on the Thursday morning. He had been interrogated during thirteen or more hours – there had been some breaks – a considerable ordeal for a man who was not a suspect in any way. Had Reid given a statement that Gleeson had buried Moll's last child, as the police tried to beat him into doing, the prosecution would have been in a quandary because it could be shown that Anastasia Cooney had arranged for the child to be interred in her family's burial plot in Kilsheelan, on the Tipperary–Waterford border.

But Tommy Reid's beating was to cause other problems during the trial. The defence had sought the barracks daybook for Monday, 25 November, listing the gardaí who had been present at the time. The judge, the prosecution and the gardaí – by now fully aligned – saw this as a 'fishing trip' to get the names of Reid's assailants. The judge refused this request and the station daybook was not handed over. This led to tetchy exchanges between the judge and the defence team, which claimed that it was being obstructed because the murder case and Reid's maltreatment were entirely separate matters. None of this helped Gleeson.

Thomas Hennessy of Knockgraffon was the next to give evidence. A man of sixty-seven years, he said that on the evening of Wednesday, 20 November, he had left his house to cycle to New Inn, sometime after 5.30 p.m. He lived down the road from the McCarthy and Lenehan cottages and so, to get to New Inn, he had taken a shortcut across the fields in a north-easterly direction, passing 'under' the Caesar farm towards the village. It was much the same route as Moll McCarthy took on her last known journey. Hennessy had to carry his bicycle across two fields and it was as he was doing this that he heard two shots, the first about eight or ten minutes after leaving his house.

The implication is that these were the shots that killed Moll McCarthy.

One of the criticisms levelled at the defence team of Nolan-Dwyer and MacBride is that they effectively allowed Hennessy's evidence to go unchallenged. He was not questioned about his hearing, for example. Marcus Bourke later learned that garda tests on Hennessy's hearing showed that it was flawed, and in some respects the man was quite deaf. It is as if the change made to the date on the charge had not happened, and that its implications – of allowing the prosecution an each-way bet on the time of death – were not fully understood. Nor did the defence appear to have understood that Hennessy could have been involved in previous attempts to get Moll McCarthy out of the district.

On the night in question, Hennessy was taking a shortcut to New Inn from where he would travel on to Cahir for a meeting of the New Inn Local Security Force B group, of which he was second in command, and which was overseen by Superintendent O'Mahony. This group's stated purpose was to help the Garda Síochána at a time when the threat of external invasion was ever-present. However, having a reserve force to back up the gardaí and the army was also seen as a means of neutralising and harnessing the energies of former members of the IRA, men who had borne arms during the War of Independence and the Civil War, and who might otherwise be drawn into supporting the guerrilla activities of other IRA activists, who saw England's difficulty as Ireland's opportunity. Another local IRA veteran, Jack Nagle, was leader of the New Inn A group, which had the more general remit of backing up the national army in case of invasion.

MacBride could not have been ignorant of these matters. He had been part of the IRA command structure that considered overtures from Fianna Fáil on this matter after the party was elected to government in 1932. He would not have needed to be told where the allegiances of prominent figures like Hennessy and Nagle lay.

Moreover, Nagle's wife, Bird Fitzgerald, was a member of one of the two Fitzgerald families in the neighbourhood of New Inn. Moll's own father was a man called Fitzgerald. Her first daughter's father was Patrick Fitzgerald. When Michael McCarthy got married many years later in London, he gave his late mother's name as Mary McCarthy, then crossed out McCarthy and substituted Fitzgerald. The defence decision not to challenge Hennessy or indeed Nagle in the witness box was a tactical one, and at this remove it is difficult to understand why it was made, unless the defence feared it might open a very awkward 'can of worms' for MacBride.

Dr James O'Connor, a general practitioner from Cashel, gave evidence to say that he had inspected

Moll's body in the stubble field at 1.15 p.m. on the Thursday she was found. She was lying flat on her back.

Mr McCarthy then questioned him for the prosecution.

> 'Did you notice her clothing?'
> 'I did. The clothing was tidily arranged, carefully arranged and it was dry.'
> 'Was there any disorder in the clothes?'
> 'On the left-hand shoulder the jacket was slightly pulled off.'

Dr O'Connor continued his evidence, saying that the dead woman's face had gone and that rigor mortis was complete. He said he placed his hand under her body and found that it was not as cold as it should have been, given rigor mortis (which sets in about three hours after death), the weather and an assumption that it had been in the field all night.[14] The body temperature was 96 degrees Fahrenheit. He told Seán MacBride that the size of the small dog found on the body would have affected the body temperature.

Dr O'Connor also noted that the way the victim's legs lay suggested that the body had been moved. MacBride seems to have missed a trick by not asking how a body thought to have been lying out in a field on a wet November night could be wearing dry clothing.

Sergeant Matthew Breen then gave evidence of finding a footprint in a field farther back on the route that Moll would have taken from her cottage to the stubble field. This proved no more than that she had recently travelled that way, wearing one of the two unmatched shoes on her when her body was found. (It was also the way to the Mass Path, the shortcut from the back of the Caesar farmhouse to New Inn church and village.)

Sergeant James Reynolds said that John Caesar's gun was found in his bedroom, along with the rod he used for cleaning it. He remarked that the gun smelled of fresh powder. Curiously, when the Garda Technical Bureau's chief firearms expert, Superintendent Daniel Stapleton, handled the gun on the Friday, the day after the body was found, no mention was made of any smell of fresh gunpowder. Stapleton, the officer in charge of the Garda Ballistics Section, gave his opinion that the first shot fired at Moll McCarthy had been from a distance of five or six feet, and the second one from about six inches away. This raised the possibility that Moll had been crossing the stubble field diagonally in a north-easterly direction, and the person who shot her could have been standing at the gap in the ditch in the adjoining field, as Gleeson said he had been doing when he spotted the body. There was also much evidence about where spent cartridges were found, but nothing to make a conclusive link between them and the crime.

In fact, it emerged that John Caesar's farm was littered with spent cartridges from his gun, to which Gleeson and others – including Sergeant Anthony Daly – had access. Stapleton's evidence continued into Friday, the fifth day of the trial, but is included here for clarity.

However, the most fascinating aspect of the ballistics evidence was not produced in court, so the jury had no way of knowing about it. In Ireland in the 1930s and 1940s, there were strict controls on the use of firearms. John Caesar was obliged to hold a licence for his shotgun. To buy cartridges, he had to go to the local authorised supplier, Feehan's hardware shop in Cashel, produce his gun licence and sign for the cartridges he bought. However, when two gardaí had called to Feehan's to inspect the firearms register, there was no entry for the sale of Eley No. 4 cartridges to Caesar in October 1940. The gardaí explained to the staff that this would not do, that they would call back in two hours and that they expected the register would be correct when they did.

The gardaí must have made their wishes clear. When they returned, an entry for 10 July 1940 had been crossed out and John Caesar, Marlhill, New Inn, was recorded as having bought 25 Eley No. 4 cartridges. His gun licence number is incorrectly recorded.[15] But even this fabrication did not match the facts already known and did not support Michael Leamy's evidence to the court that he had sold cartridges to John Caesar on 3 October 1940, when working as a shop assistant at Feehan's. We do not know what pressure Leamy came under to give his evidence. Judge Martin Maguire expressed displeasure that the firearms register was not in court, and ordered that it be sent for.

Local historian Eddie Dalton discovered this 'doctoring' in 1992 when helping Marcus Bourke to research *Murder at Marlhill*, and the book contains a photograph of the relevant entries. The arms register subsequently went missing, but photographs of the page in question, showing the alteration, are available.

A further problem was less easy to resolve. Michael Leamy had said he could not recall what size cartridges he had sold on 3 October – No. 4 or No. 5. The distinction referred to the size of the lead pellets contained within the cartridge. Typically No. 4, containing fewer, larger pellets, would be used to shoot animals like foxes, the more numerous smaller pellets of No. 5 were for shooting birds. Anyone familiar with shotguns would not have chosen No. 5 cartridges to kill a human being, as the pellets would spread over a wide area, more likely to wound rather than to kill.

The prosecution had succeeding in showing that Moll McCarthy might have been killed with Caesar's shotgun, but it failed to show that Gleeson was the one to kill her. On occasion, Gleeson had taken out the gun, hoping to encounter a marauding fox, but, not having done so, had returned it unused, and this would muddy the waters further.

It might have been different if the firearms register had been produced, as Judge Martin Maguire had very clearly ordered. The tampering would have leapt off the page and the prosecution case would have been badly holed. Both Nolan-Whelan and MacBride must share the blame for not following through on this glaring anomaly in the prosecution's case.

There is also a view among those who campaigned in recent years for a pardon for Gleeson that MacBride should have asked ballistics expert Daniel Stapleton if he weighed the shotgun pellets found in and around the body, because that would have indicated which size cartridge was used. Ironically, Dr James O'Connor, a keen sportsman who regularly bought ammunition from Feehan's hardware shop, and who would have spotted the difference in cartridge sizes in an instant, was never asked what he had seen.[16]

Stapleton's testimony was not confined to ballistics, however. He volunteered evidence that he had crossed the gap in the raised ditch while Dr McGrath, the state pathologist, was examining Moll's body in the adjoining field, saying that her head was clearly visible. This was a great bonus for the prosecution because if the superintendent could see from there who was lying in the stubble field, then so could Gleeson, a man of similar build to Stapleton.

Seán MacBride told Stapleton, a former army officer, that he was tailoring his evidence to redress weaknesses in the prosecution's case. Judge Maguire was uncharacteristically lenient in allowing MacBride to pursue this. Eventually he told MacBride to raise that point in his charge to the jury. Maguire was here inviting MacBride to challenge Stapleton's credibility when the defence summed up its case.

MacBride also made some ground in accusing Stapleton of producing evidence in the murder trial that he had withheld – 'concealed' was the word MacBride had used – at the previous hearing in the district court. At a distance of seventy-five years it is hard to disagree with MacBride but Stapleton insisted that he was telling the truth, and it was reasonable to go into more detail in a higher court. He said he was brought in as an expert witness, not aware of the prosecution case in detail, and could not be accused of trying to remedy weaknesses in it.

**DAY FIVE**

*Friday, 21 February 1941*

Seán MacBride's file on the Gleeson case contains a typescript summary of each day's proceedings. The one for the fifth day of the trial is the most dog-eared. Because he was on his feet for most of the day examining witnesses, his notes are not as informative as those for previous days. It would have been interesting to know his thinking on this day. Overall, the entire MacBride file shows meticulous, detailed preparation, particularly in cross-checking witnesses' statements for consistency. Even so, hindsight tells us that he, or his senior James Nolan-Whelan, made at least one serious tactical error.

The state pathologist, Dr John McGrath,[17] spent much of the fifth day of the trial in the witness box. In general he commanded respect from prosecuting and defending lawyers alike as being a fair-minded and reasonable witness, and his evidence was not often challenged. On this day, MacBride asked him more than 200 questions and, in doing so, got up the nose of the already irritable Judge Martin Maguire.

Underlying this was the big unsolved problem: the time of Moll McCarthy's death. The gardaí had failed to break Gleeson's alibi for the hours before he found the body. There is no suggestion that the state pathologist was complicit in this, and his evidence did not suggest that he favoured either side.

As we know, McGrath had arrived in New Inn more than twenty-four hours after Moll's body was found. He had made a superficial examination *in situ*,

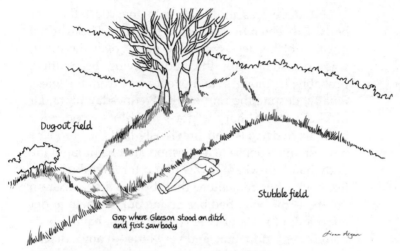

Dug-out field

Stubble field

Gap where Gleeson stood on ditch and first saw body

Moll McCarthy's body lying in the stubble field, drawn from photographs shown to the jury. Courtesy Fiona Aryan

and then he and Dr O'Connor had examined the body in greater detail at New Inn garda station.

Dr McGrath found that the victim had suffered horrific injuries from at least two gunshot wounds to the head, and had died of shock and haemorrhage. He placed the time of death at between twenty-four and forty-eight hours before 1.15 p.m. on Friday or at least fifteen hours before his examination. That wide margin effectively meant that Moll could have been killed any time between about 2 p.m. on Wednesday and about 10 a.m. on Thursday, which was around the time Gleeson reported finding the body. In other words, Dr McGrath was telling the court what was already known about the time of death. He also said that he thought the victim had died within two hours of taking her last meal, and certainly within five hours of it.

But there was more. He told the court that her body had been moved after the first shot. The artificial position of her legs, with one partly over the other, was consistent with the body having been lifted, probably, he thought, to move it away from the fence. Finally, despite the rain on the Wednesday night, Dr McGrath found that the grass and stones under the body were dry. He had previously told the coroner's inquest, in response to a question, that he thought the body had lain where it was found for anything up to ten hours. But remember that, by the time McGrath got there, the body had been lying out in a field under a tarpaulin for about twenty-four hours, having been in the open before that, and very little – if any – drying could be expected in damp November weather.

From Dr McGrath's evidence, the jury learned much about Moll McCarthy and what had caused her death. She was a well-built woman of about forty years, five feet five inches tall and between nine and ten stone. She was killed by the first shot. It hit her neck on the left-hand side, severing her carotid artery, and her death would have been almost instant. This shot was fired horizontally from a distance of about five or six feet. After she fell, a second gunshot was fired down at her from closer range (about six inches according to Superintendent Stapleton) and took away her face.

The victim had been wearing a woollen coat and a skirt, with a brown shoe on her right foot and a black shoe on the left one. Dr McGrath believed that her coat had been buttoned up after she had been killed, because there were bloodstains on the inside of the coat. When her body was found, her legs were crossed and her skirt band (a form of belt) had been tied, also possibly after her death. Her underwear was largely undisturbed, and the state pathologist did not find any signs of a sexual assault. An internal examination suggested to him that she had had sexual intercourse with a man between twenty-four and sixty hours before her death, though he thought sixty hours was at the outside boundary of probability.

What both doctors agreed upon unconditionally was that Moll McCarthy was killed by the first shot, and killed almost instantly. This meant the second shot which blew away her face was fired after she was already dead. It was an act of considerable savagery – and may hold a clue to the motivations of the person responsible.

Dr McGrath said that he had had Moll's little black dog put down, and had examined the remains, but the dog's stomach was virtually empty and he had learned little from the exercise. In response to questions, he said that it was possible that the presence of the dog on top of the body had slowed down the cooling of the body, but the authorities he had consulted were ambiguous on how much effect this would have had. He had experimented by placing a basin of hot water on another dead body, but had reached no useful conclusion. The state pathologist was careful in his evidence not to challenge Dr O'Connor's readings – he simply offered his opinion based on the measurements he had taken himself, and his own wide experience. The prosecution did not challenge Dr O'Connor's high temperature reading.

McGrath's other findings concerned the state of the body. He found about two dozen lead shotgun pellets near it. There were cartridge wads in Moll's clothes, her neck was peppered with pellet marks and one cartridge wad had wedged in her hair. Apart from her coat being torn, her clothes had not been damaged. Judge Martin Maguire asked Dr McGrath about the bloodstains inside Moll's coat:

> 'Would that indicate that the coat had been buttoned after the stains came there?'
>
> 'It would, particularly as while there were stains and particles of tissue on the inside of the coat, the stains on the pullover underneath did not correspond to the stains on the underside of the coat.'

Marcus Bourke suggested that the significance of that eluded everyone at the trial. How can one die of head and facial injuries and have blood on the inside of a buttoned coat, blood that has not soaked through from the outside? The defence failed miserably to draw the obvious conclusion. Moll McCarthy had been assaulted elsewhere, possibly after being given a punishment beating, and her clothes were replaced on her dead body *before* it was carried to a nearby field. In fact, there was evidence that more than just her coat had been replaced. And what sort of person or persons could have done this? Who could kill a woman with one shot, button her into her coat and carry her body into an open field, probably with assistance, and then fire another shot which takes away her face?

Dr McGrath was asked about the contents of Moll's stomach. 'It contained half a pint or more of semi-fluid material which appeared to be partially digested bread and tea,' he said. The womb appeared of normal size and there was no indication of pregnancy. He later said that a small meal, such as bread and tea, usually leaves the stomach in three to five hours. 'For that reason, I say that death probably took place within two hours of taking that meal,' Dr McGrath said.

He was asked if he had examined the victim's vagina.

> 'Yes. It contained some seminoid fluid … on later examination, I found in it a number of complete typical spermatozoa … I concluded that it was probable that the fluid came into the vagina within about twenty-four hours before death and up to, say, sixty hours.'
>
> 'Was there any blood in the body?'
> 'It was very little.'

The jury was never told where the blood went. It should have been in the body or where the body was lying. We know – because the state pathologist and Dr O'Connor told us – that it did not pump or leak out on to her clothing. The blood could have been where she was killed – it could have been in Lynch's disused farmhouse nearby or in some other place where Moll had gone to meet a man on the Wednesday evening. People who wish to have sex on rainy late November evenings do not make assignations to meet in partially ploughed fields when there are disused farmhouses in reasonably good condition within easy reach.

Under further questioning, Dr McGrath said
that if one assumed that Moll McCarthy had been
shot between 5 p.m. and 6 p.m. on the Wednesday,
he would regard Dr O'Connor's finding of her
body temperature as 96 degrees Fahrenheit to be
'inexplicable'.

The prosecution was making the case that the two
shots heard by Thomas Hennessy on Wednesday
about 6 p.m. were the shots that killed Moll.

For the defence, McBride asked McGrath if he
really thought that the presence of the dog crouched
on Moll's chest could have distorted the temperature
readings. Had the fact of sudden death affected the
speed of cooling of the body? McGrath's answer
was inconclusive – it might, but, then again, it might
not. However, he did say that exceptional cases had
occurred, and cited research by Professor Sydney
Smith, professor of forensic medicine at the University
of Edinburgh, and from *Taylor's Medical Jurisprudence*,
a standard text. He said that the presence of the little
dog on the deceased's abdomen could have kept
the body warmer than might be expected, but the
obvious conclusion from Dr O'Connor's test was that
Moll McCarthy had died one or two hours before
his examination. However, Dr O'Connor found that
the state of rigor mortis utterly contradicted the
temperature finding.

What if one ignored Dr O'Connor's temperature
finding? 'From [my] examination of rigor mortis
I would say that the death took place 15 hours before
the time of my examination [this was around 1 p.m.
on the Friday or 27 hours after the body was found]
… and from the temperature as I found it, death took

place 24 to 48 hours before I took the temperature,'
Dr McGrath said. (As the body was discovered
around 10 a.m. on Thursday, McGrath's finding of
time of death based on rigor mortis tells us nothing,
and that based on temperature is so vague as to be of
little help.)

Dr McGrath said he had examined Harry Gleeson's
clothing, which the gardaí had taken from him when
they had questioned him for the second time, and
found semen stains on the bottom of a shirt, and on
the inside of a trouser leg. He also found an oxblood
stain. In reply to MacBride, the state pathologist said
that finding semen stains on clothing that a man had
worn for a week or so did not prove that there had
been sexual contact with a woman.

Under further cross-examination, MacBride got
McGrath to say that if Dr O'Connor's temperature
reading was correct, death could not have taken
place around 6.30 p.m. on Wednesday evening, as the
prosecution maintained. He also got McGrath to agree
that if one disregarded the presence of the dog, the
time of death could have been within an hour or two of
Dr O'Connor's examination on the Thursday morning.

MacBride had done well, but he had not reckoned
on Judge Maguire having the last word. 'From your
examination of the body and your post-mortem
examination of the body was there anything inconsistent with the condition of the body with this
woman having been shot between 5.30 and 6 p.m. on
Wednesday November, 20th?' Maguire asked.

The court report typescript shows that the pathologist answered, 'Yes.' However, this has been over-
typed with 'No' typed in its place. In fact, Maguire

had asked a trick question, along the lines of 'when did you stop beating your wife?' The problem with the question is that it asked McGrath to ignore all the conflicting evidence, principally but not exclusively that of Dr O'Connor. 'From your examination of the body and your post-mortem examination …' The state pathologist was bound to reply truthfully, but had the question been asked minus the qualifying phrase, the answer was yes; of course there were lots of reasons why the state pathologist could not definitely identify around 5.30 to 6 p.m. on Wednesday as the time of death. The jury heard only the answer, but did not notice the earlier qualifications that make the given answer meaningless. Maguire's job as judge was to stop lawyers pulling stunts like that, not to use them himself.

Now, having heard the evidence given by the two doctors who had examined Moll McCarthy's body, the jury was none the wiser about the time of her death – and more than seventy years later, neither are we. Was she the victim of a punishment beating that went too far, and the later shot removing her face was intended to conceal that? There was no bruising to her arms and legs or her torso, suggesting that she knew her assailant(s) and did not put up a struggle.

We do know that her body was moved after she was killed – both doctors agreed on that – but we don't know what distance: inches, feet or yards. And if she was moved from a disused farmhouse or another nearby hiding place, then more than one person had to have been involved.

## DAY SIX

*Saturday, 22 February 1941*

There were two witnesses for the prosecution on the morning of 22 February and the most significant was Superintendent Patrick O'Mahony of Cahir, the officer in charge of the garda investigation into Moll McCarthy's murder.[18]

First, Inspector Thomas O'Reilly of Thurles garda station resumed giving evidence, having briefly begun the previous day. When making a statement on 25 November, Gleeson had asked if the gardaí had fixed a time for the death of Moll McCarthy and was told they had not. After the statement was completed, Gleeson had mentioned putting a sack on the field pump in October to stop the water from freezing, but he had noticed that it had gone missing on 19 November. This bag was to be central to Superintendent O'Mahony's evidence later. Not for the first time, gardaí had added useful material for the prosecution case in the form of a preface – Gleeson's inquiry about the time of death – and a postscript – the missing sack – to statements the defendant had made. It was, we are to believe, O'Mahony's great good fortune that Gleeson voluntarily mentioned the missing sack after the Friday nine-hour interrogation had finished, just too late for it to be included in his signed statement.

When he took the stand, Superintendent O'Mahony said that on Tuesday, 26 November, he went with Gleeson to the McCarthy home to see if they could locate the missing sack.

There – according to O'Mahony – a conversation took place between Gleeson and Moll's eldest sons

Patrick and Michael, with O'Mahony listening and making notes and eventually intervening to bring it to a close. The presence of Moll's sons at the cottage was contrived by O'Mahony. Otherwise Patrick should have been at work on Hanley's farm, and Michael was supposed to be in care.

*Michael*: 'What are you looking for, Harry?'
*Gleeson*: 'A bag that was taken off the pump.'

[In winter, outdoor pumps were wrapped with hessian sacks or bags to keep them from freezing.]

*Michael*: 'What about the bag my mother gave you on Tuesday [19 November, the day before Moll disappeared].'
*Gleeson*: 'I got no bag from your mother on Tuesday.'
*Michael* (*pointing his finger at Gleeson*): 'You did, you did, you did.'
*Gleeson*: 'Tuesday evening … what time?'
*Michael*: 'Didn't she tell me she gave you a bag some time on Tuesday?'
*Gleeson*: 'She told you … I wasn't speaking to your mother high or dry on Tuesday.'
*Michael*: 'You were. She gave you a bag and don't be telling lies. You were to give her potatoes in it near the dug-out on Wednesday night.'
*Gleeson*: 'I wasn't speaking to your mother on Tuesday. I saw her about half one. She was spancelling [hobbling] goats in the field.'
*Michael*: 'She did give you the bag and she went out on Wednesday night to get potatoes from you, because you were to get them for her

while the old people [John and Bridget Caesar] were in Cashel or somewhere, and you are the father of the last child too.'

*Gleeson*: 'Who can prove that?'

*Patrick*: 'You are the father of the last child, Harry. My mother told me.'

*Gleeson*: 'People could tell lies. Your mother could be telling you things and it might be other people.'

*Michael*: 'You are the father of the last child, you are, you are, you are.'

*Gleeson to Patrick*: 'Had I ever an angry word with you, sonny?'

*Patrick*: 'You had not.'

*Michael*: 'But you had with my mother when she said you were the father of the last child.'

*Gleeson*: 'Who is to prove that?'

*Patrick*: 'My mother said it.'

*Gleeson*: 'Did I ever take out a knife to you, Mickey?'

*Michael*: 'You did over near the boreen.'

*Gleeson*: 'Did I open it?'

*Michael*: 'You did and you followed me with it and you said you'd cut off my head.'

*Gleeson*: 'That was when you were young. 'Twas a joke.'

*Patrick*: 'You followed him with a knife all right.'

*Michael*: 'You were the father of the last child – you're letting on not to be. You needn't be laughing.'

*Gleeson to Patrick*: 'Didn't I get rabbits from you?'

*Patrick*: 'You did.'

*Gleeson*: 'Didn't I pay you for them?'

*Patrick*: 'You did.'

*Michael*:   'My mother said you were the father of the last child. You can't deny it.'

*Gleeson*:   'She could tell you many a thing.'

*Michael*:   'She did, and you told her to keep her mouth shut about it. You can hit me now for saying that, but you're afraid.'

*Gleeson*:   'Did I ever hit you?'

*Michael*:   'You did. She gave you the bag last Tuesday, and I saw it above in the house [he means Caesar's farmyard] yesterday.'

*Gleeson*:   'There is no bag belonging to you above, but if you think there is, go up and get it. I never got a bag from your mother.'

*Michael*:   'You did and you were to give her potatoes in it on Wednesday night.'

*Gleeson to Patrick*: 'Did you ever see me giving potatoes to your mother?'

*Patrick*:   'I often did.'

*Gleeson*:   'What about all the potatoes that were taken out of the pit?'

*Patrick*:   'Do you remember the night my mother and myself were down at the snares? You took her down the field for them. You told me to stay where I was and when she came back she had a butt of potatoes. You often gave her potatoes.'

*Gleeson*:   'Your mother was a liar. The Lord have mercy on her soul.'

*Superintendent O'Mahony*: 'Moll is dead, better not be talking like that about her.'

*Michael*:   'She is dead.'

At this point, O'Mahony said he had noticed that Michael was crying, and he ended the confrontation.

There was no other witness to this conversation, although Inspector O'Reilly had accompanied O'Mahony to the McCarthy cottage. O'Mahony had produced what he said was a 'verbatim note' of what was said. The salient points of this alleged conversation were that Michael said that his mother had given Gleeson a sack on Tuesday, the day before she went missing, that Moll and Gleeson had arranged to meet at the dug-out field the next day (Wednesday) to hand over the sack filled with potatoes – the implication was that this was a payment for sex – while John and Bridget Caesar were in Cashel for fair day. Gleeson denied getting a bag from Moll and denied having seen her after 1.30 p.m. on that day, in O'Mahony's account of the exchange between him and the McCarthy boys.

Gleeson's counsel twice objected to this evidence. Nolan-Whelan said the conversation had not been put to the boys when they were giving evidence and Superintendent O'Mahony's notes did not constitute good evidence.

A further legal wrangle about the admissibility of the O'Mahony account of the exchange followed, with the judge appearing to rule that if Gleeson 'adopted the account of the exchange' – in other words, acknowledged that it was correct – then it could be admitted. Nolan-Whelan argued that the defendant was being prejudiced by the very fact of the disputed evidence being presented. The evidence of the McCarthy boys was being given for them by a policeman, and they had not been asked in the witness box to say whether or not the 'verbatim' account was correct.

Earlier at the committal stage, Seán MacBride had similarly objected and Judge Seán Troy had said that it was a matter for the trial judge to decide on. At the subsequent appeal, the chief justice expressed dissatisfaction with the way this evidence had been handled by the trial judge, Martin Maguire, but held that this was not sufficient grounds to overturn the jury's verdict.

Note that in this retelling of this alleged conversation, O'Mahony told the court that Michael McCarthy had said that Gleeson had given potatoes to Moll, when previously Michael had said he had never seen this happen. MacBride's notes suggest that he doubted if this exchange ever took place, and we have only O'Mahony's word for it. The prosecution could have called Inspector O'Reilly, who was at Moll McCarthy's cottage at the time this exchange was said to have happened. It is also possible that Michael may have thought he was being accused of stealing a bag. This is not as far-fetched as it might appear. The McCarthy children were often accused of thieving. If anything went missing, they got the blame, whether or not they were guilty.

Nor did it help that this 'evidence' was presented on a Saturday morning, but the defence cross-examination of O'Mahony was left to the following Monday. The jury went home just after 1.30 p.m. for what was left of the weekend with this supposed conversation fresh in their minds.

Over the previous six days, they had heard the prosecution's case in a horrific murder but had heard nothing in Harry Gleeson's favour. The following week, they would hear the brief case for the defence, but what they had already heard must have seemed very persuasive.

**DAY SEVEN**

## *Monday, 24 February 1941*

Two witnesses took up a whole day's proceedings as the second and final week of the trial began. First, Superintendent O'Mahony was back in the witness box to be cross-examined by Mr Nolan-Whelan about the evidence he had given two days earlier.

Nolan-Whelan began by challenging the policeman's new 'evidence' about the onset of rigor mortis in Moll McCarthy's body when he had first seen it (new in the sense that he had not adverted to it in the committal hearing).

O'Mahony said: 'I touched the left hand and the toe of the right shoe. I just stirred it.'

'Could you feel the toe through the shoe?' Nolan-Whelan asked.

'I could not, but I felt the movement of the whole leg. I know nothing about rigor mortis. All I know is that when I touched it, it was stiff and when I touched the right shoe, the leg appeared to be stiff.'

O'Mahony agreed that he had not mentioned this in the earlier court hearing, saying that this was because it was normal to give more detailed evidence in murder trials.

Nolan-Whelan pursued the point. O'Mahony was now giving evidence of the onset of rigor mortis in the body, evidence that was properly the preserve of the two expert witnesses, the doctors who examined the body, and who could not agree on the time of death.

'I put it to you' Nolan-Whelan said, 'that you realised the danger [to the prosecution case] of the time being placed after 5 to 6 p.m. on the Wednesday night and in consequence you brought out this additional evidence.'

'I did not; that is not correct.'

Nolan-Whelan then turned to O'Mahony's statement taken from Gleeson on Monday, 25 November. As we saw earlier, Gleeson gave two statements to the gardaí, one on the day after Moll's body was found, and a much longer one on the following Monday, 25 November. This second statement – taken over the course of thirteen hours – is the subject of the following exchange.

'You gave him the usual caution?' Nolan-Whelan asked O'Mahony.

'Yes.'

'If you said to a person who had previously made a lengthy statement [as Gleeson had done the previous Friday to Inspector O'Reilly] that you were going to ask him some questions, would that person be under the impression that some questions meant some additional questions, accounting for a limited time, say half an hour?'

O'Mahony replied that he could not say how anyone would look at it.

Later, O'Mahony denied having had anything to do with Gleeson being detained in a cell in Limerick jail with two unrelated prisoners called Ryan, although he admitted visiting the prison and questioning the Ryans. Outside the court, gardaí were saying that Gleeson had incriminated himself in conversation with the two Ryans while sharing a cell with them in Limerick, but the Ryans were never asked to give evidence.

O'Mahony added that Gleeson had been moved from the shared cell before he [O'Mahony] had the opportunity to question his cellmates.

Nolan-Whelan was here trying to alert the jury to the fact that O'Mahony had been party to a failed scheme to trick Gleeson into 'confessing' to his cellmates.

Nolan-Whelan then questioned O'Mahony over the way in which he had produced a 'verbatim' note of the contested exchange between Gleeson and the two eldest McCarthy boys given in Saturday's evidence. The superintendent admitted that two pages of his notes were no longer available. He said that, on the day the confrontation occurred, he did not have his official notebook with him, and that he had used a copybook, out of which he had later torn the pages, when putting together his finished account of the exchange.

There was another way of looking at this. If O'Mahony had really recorded the exchange between Gleeson and the two McCarthy brothers as it happened, it would be in his notebook for the correct day and time and in the correct sequence. However, if it had been concocted at a later date, it would be out of place and therefore open to challenge.

A major problem for the jury was that either they believed the garda superintendent and the two boys, though the brothers had given no evidence on this point, or they believed Harry Gleeson. By then, the jury had probably concluded that Gleeson went to Moll for the same services as most of the other men for miles around. In the jury's eyes, it looked as if this was the word of a truthful if possibly mistaken prosecution witness against that of an untruthful accused person. Gleeson was always going to lose that contest. The jury did not know that Superintendent O'Mahony was the bigger liar.

But Nolan-Whelan could have made more of O'Mahony's tactic of giving other people's evidence for them plus his attempt to give evidence about the onset of rigor mortis in the corpse, despite claiming to know nothing about it.

The cross-examination concluded with a circular argument about the effects of the mistake in Garda Quinlan's scene of the crime map where the corpse was placed in the wrong position in the field. The net point of this exchange was that if Quinlan's map had been correct in where it placed Moll McCarthy's body, Gleeson must have recognised her when he looked over the gap into the field where it was lying.

Since Moll's face had been damaged beyond recognition by the second gunshot and the view of her face from the gap in the ditch was hidden by the dog crouched on her body, the point seems moot at this remove. Moll would be recognised by her hair, her clothes and general shape, or not at all. The most likely explanation is that Gleeson did have a pretty good idea about the identity of the body he had seen lying in the field. But even if he had recognised Moll and subsequently denied it, while this damages the credibility of his evidence, it does not prove that he was the murderer.

That ended the prosecution case. Mr Nolan-Whelan asked the judge to make a ruling on the admissibility of Superintendent O'Mahony's evidence about the exchange between Gleeson and Patrick and Michael McCarthy.

The judge said that Superintendent O'Mahony's evidence contained allegations that had been denied. 'You may take it that I will be at particular trouble to explain to the jury that these statements are merely allegations or charges, as distinct from proof on matters laid. As a matter of fact, the jury know all that as well as any one of us but I will keep you right.' Here Maguire told Nolan-Whelan that he, as judge, would warn the jury of the flaws in this second-hand way of putting very damning evidence in the boys' mouths.

It was now coming up to 11.30 a.m. Seán MacBride made the opening presentation for the defence, which continued until 1.30 p.m. After lunch, he resumed his address to the jury and concluded at 4.15 p.m. when Gleeson took the stand and was examined by Nolan-Whelan.

We have a good account of MacBride's presentation of the defence because it was published in the *Clonmel Nationalist* on Saturday, 2 March. In it, MacBride said that very little of the prosecution case against Gleeson remained standing. The prosecution had suggested a three-part motive: Gleeson was the father of the deceased child Peggy; he was having a continuing immoral relationship with Moll McCarthy; and she was blackmailing him by threatening to tell John Caesar about their relationship. If any one of those elements failed, the others became meaningless. The only shred of evidence that Gleeson was Peggy's father had come from Michael McCarthy, who said that he had heard his mother say to Gleeson that she would bring him to law about that child. Michael admitted that he was some distance away from his mother when this was said, and Gleeson had no recollection of the contention having been made. MacBride maintained that the suggestion had been dragged in to poison the minds of jurors against his client. He dismissed the conversation between Michael and Patrick McCarthy and Gleeson as having been engineered by O'Mahony, and asked why the boys had not been asked about it when they had given evidence. He suggested that they would not swear to it because it was not true.

MacBride also asked if the jury really believed that Moll McCarthy, who had kept the paternity of her last child a secret, would have told her two young sons the name of the father of that child. He said that Anastasia Cooney, a charitable woman of independent means, had tried to help Moll spiritually and materially. Miss Cooney had said that Moll would not tell her who the father was, that she had suspicions of her own, but Moll would neither confirm nor deny them. In the event, Miss Cooney was not called to give evidence, though she was present in court throughout the trial.

MacBride told the jury that not a shred of evidence had been put forward to support the notion of Gleeson having a sexual relationship with Moll McCarthy. The only evidence given of a relationship had them talking across a fence separating them, and that Gleeson had been seen beckoning to her because he wanted to speak to her. No evidence had been offered to support the notion that she was blackmailing him.

Anyone in the neighbourhood of Marlhill could have killed Moll McCarthy, MacBride said. Gleeson would have been very unlikely to kill her on his own doorstep. If he really wanted to get rid of her, surely he would have lured her to a remote place, and not one associated with him?

As regards means, the prosecution had suggested that Moll was shot with a gun using Eley No. 5 shot.[19] As against that, they had Superintendent Stapleton's evidence that similar guns to that of John Caesar were to be found in almost every farmhouse in County Tipperary. MacBride also appealed to the jury to note the way the prosecution had presented its case, suggesting that Gleeson was guilty unless he could prove that he was innocent. 'One would think that the rule of law – that the accused was presumed innocent until proved guilty – had been reversed in this case.'

MacBride continued: 'If there is one thing more important than another in a murder case, it is the position of the body of the person who had been murdered. A map was prepared by a mapping expert for the purpose of this case. On it was indicated a point A which showed where a sod of earth had been removed by the authorities. On that sod had laid the head of Mary McCarthy and it has now been proved that the point A was marked on the wrong side of the gap in the field where the body was discovered. According to that map, the head of Mary McCarthy was placed at a point forty feet from the corner of the field, whereas Dr McGrath, the state pathologist, said the head of the deceased woman was twenty-seven feet from the corner of the field.'

MacBride told the jury that they would have to decide if that map had been an honest mistake, or an attempt to mislead them into believing Harry Gleeson to be guilty. He said he was amazed that the prosecution had not withdrawn the map when the mistake was revealed. He continued: 'There was practically no blood around the place where the body was found, and Dr McGrath has said that he did not find as much blood under the head as he would have expected. If Mary McCarthy had been shot in the neck near the gap, as the prosecution alleged, there should have been a considerable amount of blood at the place, but no trace was found there. That was rather amazing.'

The position of Mary McCarthy's clothes suggested that she had been carried by the arms from some other location and placed in the field in a dead or dying condition. The night was wet but her clothes were dry. There was mud on the back of her coat, yet the ground beneath her was dry. Where did the mud come from? (Here MacBride is trying to square an inexplicable circle – if the ground was dry, the clothes should logically have been wet, yet neither clothes nor ground were wet, according to the evidence.) And what about the bloodstains inside the victim's coat with no corresponding marks on the outside?

MacBride then began to try to disentangle the evidence of the two doctors who had examined the body. The first on the scene, Dr O'Connor, had found an internal body temperature that was almost normal for a living human being. The timing of the onset of rigor mortis was an unreliable indicator of time of death, he said.

The prosecution case was that Mary McCarthy was killed by the two shots heard by Thomas Hennessy after 5.30 p.m. on the Wednesday; the defence contended that the medical evidence pointed to the death having occurred after 6 a.m. on the Thursday.

Two witnesses, Michael McCarthy and Tommy Reid, were much closer to where the body was found than Thomas Hennessy was on the Wednesday evening, and neither said anything about hearing shots at that time.

As far as Reid's evidence was concerned, MacBride said it should be accepted or rejected *in toto*. The prosecution was asking the jury to believe the bits it found helpful, and reject those that did not suit its case. If Reid was prepared to commit perjury, why did he not finish the job and give Gleeson a complete alibi?

Turning to John Caesar's shotgun, MacBride told the court that Superintendent Reynolds had said it smelled of fresh powder, but Superintendent Stapleton, the firearms expert, had made no mention of fresh powder. Stapleton suggested that a number of shots had been fired from the gun. 'How far does that take us?' MacBride asked.

Returning to the flawed map, MacBride said that the defence would shortly call Patrick Munden, a well-known Dublin architect, who had produced an accurate map of the field where the body lay, based on uncontested measurements taken by the state pathologist. Munden would give evidence that, from Gleeson's vantage point, he could not have seen the woman's head. If the dog was lying on the body, as Gleeson had said, then all he would have seen was the dog and the woman's legs. And Munden would prove that Michael McCarthy, who said he could see Gleeson crossing the gap with his dog, could have only seen a man's head, and that the twelve-year-old was either telling lies or was confused, MacBride concluded.

The jury finally had its first real chance to get the measure of Harry Gleeson when he took the stand at 4.15 p.m. Previously, all he had said was 'I had neither hand, act nor part in the murder of Mary McCarthy' in reply to the charge read to him at the beginning of the trial. Since then, he had sat impassively in the dock hearing some of the evidence, and not hearing other passages, according to a person present throughout.[20]

The jury saw a well-built, dark-haired man nearly six feet tall, aged about forty, an outdoor man. He would spend the rest of Monday and most of the following day giving evidence, spending longer in the witness box than anyone else. We do not have an account of his demeanour, but the record of his responses to almost a thousand questions suggests a man who was in control of himself, ready to respond to searching questions.

He was questioned first by his own lead counsel, James Nolan-Whelan, and confirmed the two lengthy statements he had given to gardaí, saying that they were made before he had engaged legal representation. Judge Maguire intervened to contradict this, but Nolan-Whelan quickly showed that the judge was wrong. Gleeson also confirmed that he denied the allegations against him made in Superintendent O'Mahony's account of the exchange with the McCarthy boys. He did confirm being present when the conversation had taken place. He went on to say that Moll McCarthy had not accused him of being the father of her last child. He had last taken out John Caesar's gun a week before Moll McCarthy's death because he had seen a fox making off with a goose on the Widow Fitzgerald's field. Here is an important point lost in subsequent discussion of the case – Gleeson said he had taken out the gun, not that he had fired it. Gleeson described his regime for training the greyhound that he had with him, and how it differed from that of the other dogs on the farm. The ownership of the greyhound was not mentioned.

Nolan-Whelan asked his client fewer than forty questions, and the most significant was the final exchange.

*Nolan-Whelan*: Were you the father of Mary
McCarthy's last child?
*Gleeson*: No, sir, I only heard it.
*Nolan-Whelan*: Had you at any time any immoral
or improper association with Mary
McCarthy?
*Gleeson*: No, sir.
*Nolan-Whelan*: Had you any hand, act or part in the
killing of Mary McCarthy?
*Gleeson*: No, sir.

Given the volume of the evidence produced against him earlier, it seems odd that Nolan-Whelan did not question his client longer, giving Gleeson an opportunity to present himself in his own words to the jury as an innocent man. Nolan-Whelan's interrogation lasted a little over an hour.

Then it was the prosecution's turn. Joseph A. McCarthy began by asking Gleeson if he was deaf. Gleeson said that he was, and if he had a cold the condition was worse. The judge intervened to say that Gleeson was clearly hearing everything that was said to him. 'Well, you heard that question and I didn't hear it,' observed Maguire.

Gleeson explained to counsel that he found it easier to hear someone who was standing up, but as the questioning continued, it became clear that Gleeson was not hearing everything, or was doing a good job of pretending not to hear. There has been some speculation since the trial that Gleeson had been taking tablets that had been prescribed for an aunt; it was common enough in rural Ireland for medication to be informally shared.

There followed an inconsequential exchange between prosecution counsel and Gleeson about whether, more than twelve years previously, Moll McCarthy had visited John Caesar's previous farm at Graigue, a townland close to Marlhill, where Gleeson had also lived. It is not clear now, and looks likely that it was not clear then, what point the prosecution was trying to make. Did prosecution counsel mean to suggest that Moll McCarthy had visited Caesar and/or Gleeson at Graigue for immoral purposes?

More pertinent questioning focused on Moll McCarthy's recent pattern of visits to the Caesar farm, generally twice a week to get water; who the other female visitors to the Caesar farm were; and if Gleeson knew the colour of Moll McCarthy's last dog. The suggestion was that Gleeson should have recognised the dog, if not the woman on whose body it was crouched.

The subject turned to Gleeson's actions on the morning he found Moll's body. 'You came down on the morning of the 21st of November. You had been out sometime?' McCarthy asked. 'I was out since a quarter past seven,' Gleeson replied. [NB He is using 'old time'.]

*McCarthy*:  'Where were you from a quarter past
seven to a quarter to nine?'

*Gleeson*:  'I had breakfast to take.'

*McCarthy*:  'How long did that take?'

*Gleeson*:  'Ten or twelve minutes, then I had the
horses to let in.'

*McCarthy*:  'Where did you go then?'

*Gleeson*:  'I let in the horses and fed them in the
house. [He meant the yard.] I brought
them from the fields.'

*McCarthy*:  'What time would that be?'

*Gleeson*:  'Anything from 7.30 o'clock.'

*McCarthy*:  'At that time, you didn't hear any shot?'

*Gleeson*:  'No.'

*McCarthy*:  'After you fed the horses, what did you do?'

*Gleeson*:  'I went over milking the cows, sir.'

*McCarthy*:  'Where?'

*Gleeson*:  'Over the passage down the boreen.'
[This was the path leading in a westerly
direction from Caesar's house to the main
road.]

*McCarthy*:  'Did you go down the pump field?'

*Gleeson*:  'Yes, sir.'

*McCarthy*:  'How long were you with the horses?'

*Gleeson*:  'The horses would not take long – about
five minutes.'

*McCarthy*:  'So at twenty-five minutes to eight o'clock,
you went down the lane to the pump field?'

*Gleeson*:  'Yes.'

*McCarthy*:  'When you were going down the lane, I
think you were three fields away from the
dug-out?'

*Gleeson*:  'Yes, sir.'

*McCarthy*: 'And from twenty-five minutes to eight o'clock while you were out, did you hear any shot?'

Before Gleeson answered, the judge intervened to ask Gleeson if he had heard any shots that morning.

*Gleeson*: 'No, sir.'

*McCarthy*: 'You began in the pump field milking cows?'

*Gleeson*: 'Yes.'

*McCarthy*: 'What time did you leave that?'

*Gleeson*: 'It would be shoving towards half past eight o'clock or thereabouts.'

*Judge*: 'That would leave you in the pump field almost an hour?'

*Gleeson*: 'I would not know. I would be milking that time. I might be there anything from half an hour to an hour.'

*McCarthy*: 'Anyway, you were in the pump field long before five minutes to nine o'clock. Had you a view from where you were milking the cows of Mary McCarthy's house and yard?'

*Gleeson*: 'I had, sir.'

*McCarthy*: 'Were you looking in that direction?'

*Gleeson*: 'I could not be doing that when doing the milking.'

*McCarthy*: 'Then you were not ... did you look in that direction?'

*Gleeson*: 'No, sir.'

*McCarthy*: 'So Michael McCarthy saw you from the yard there at five minutes to eight o'clock,

| | |
|---|---|
| | looking in your direction and you did not see him?' |
| *Gleeson*: | 'No, sir.' |
| *McCarthy*: | 'How far away from where you were looking was McCarthy's cottage?' |
| *Gleeson*: | 'I suppose it would be three to four hundred yards.' |
| *McCarthy*: | 'So then you went back again, I take it, to the house [i.e. Caesar's farmhouse]?' |
| *Gleeson*: | 'Yes, sir.' |
| *McCarthy*: | 'And then you came back again about the back of Gorman's [field]?' |
| *Gleeson*: | 'Yes, sir.' |

The jury had earlier heard evidence about the lie of the land in the area where Gleeson found the body. Close to the corner adjoining O'Gorman's field, there was a raised ditch separating two of Caesar's fields. Closest to the farmhouse was the dug-out field. A raised ditch separated it from the stubble field where Gleeson had been ploughing the previous day. Gleeson now gave evidence of being in the dug-out field looking for the bull and the sheep. He jumped up on the ditch and saw a body on the other side. Sometimes this ditch was referred to as a fence, but photographs show a more informal barrier between the two fields, a mound of raised earth and hedging. The ground was almost a foot lower in the next field, the stubble field where the body was lying.

| | |
|---|---|
| *McCarthy*: | 'You put your hand on the fence. Will you show us now here and you stood at the fence?' |

*Gleeson*: 'Show me the map and I will show you.'

*McCarthy*: 'No, show it here.'

*Gleeson*: 'I had a dog [meaning the greyhound] in my right hand, and I would be going straight to the fence and I had one hand on the ditch and my foot on the step, and when I looked over the ditch, a dog growled at me and I gave a look and I saw a woman.'

*McCarthy*: 'You looked over the fence first?'

*Gleeson*: 'Yes.'

*McCarthy*: 'And the dog growled at you?'

*Gleeson*: 'Yes.'

*McCarthy*: 'Did you make any noise?'

*Gleeson*: 'No, sir.'

*McCarthy*: 'So that you made no noise but the dog growled at you?'

*Gleeson*: 'When I came at him in a hurry and he saw me, he growled.'

*McCarthy*: 'But you came from the other side of Gorman's pound [field]?'

*Gleeson*: 'Yes.'

*McCarthy*: 'And then you said you looked out. How long did you look out?'

*Gleeson*: 'When the dog growled at me, I gave a look and the dog growled and I doubled back again and turned.'

*Judge*: 'Why did you do that?'

*Gleeson*: 'I could not go out [he appears to mean go on across the ditch] and I having a hound with me. I looked out and seen the woman and doubled [back] off the ditch.' [As stated earlier, Gleeson had two other

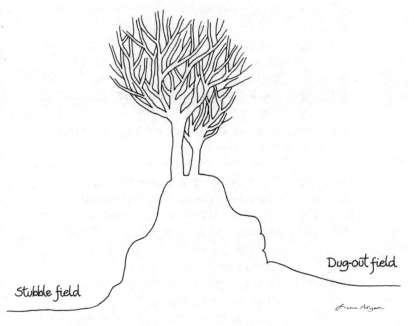

Cross-section view of ditch separating fields. The body lay in the field
on the left. Drawn to scale from court exhibit. Courtesy Fiona Aryan

|           | farm dogs with him, but his concern here was about controlling the greyhound.] |
|-----------|--------------------------------------------------------------------------------|
| *McCarthy*: | 'Why did you go away and leave a woman lying there?' |
| *Gleeson*: | 'I came to the conclusion it was the best thing to do.' |
| *McCarthy*: | 'When you looked out at the woman, she was, according to Superintendent Stapleton's evidence, about eight feet, eleven inches away from your eye. Would that be about right?' |
| *Gleeson*: | 'I cannot tell, sir.' |

| | |
|---|---|
| *McCarthy*: | 'Right underneath you?' |
| *Gleeson*: | 'Underneath me mostly.' |
| *McCarthy*: | 'And you saw the dog you said as in your statement it was lying on her chest?' |
| *Gleeson*: | 'Yes, sir.' |
| *McCarthy*: | 'You knew Mary McCarthy?' |
| *Gleeson*: | 'Yes, sir.' |
| *McCarthy*: | 'How far away was her chest from her chin?' |
| *Gleeson*: | 'I don't understand you.' |
| *McCarthy*: | 'Show us where you saw the dog.' |
| *Gleeson*: | 'About here [indicating his own chest].' |
| *McCarthy*: | 'And you tell the twelve gentlemen of the jury that you saw the dog's head that way and you saw nothing else?' |
| *Gleeson*: | 'I didn't, sir.' |
| *McCarthy*: | 'How did you know that this woman was either dead or sleeping?' |
| *Gleeson*: | 'This was the conclusion I came to when I seen her lying.' |
| *McCarthy*: | 'How did you come to that conclusion?' |
| *Gleeson*: | 'When I seen her lying down there.' |
| *McCarthy*: | 'You thought of what you were going to do?' |
| *Gleeson*: | 'No, the conclusion was when I came to the fence, the impression I got was the woman was either sleeping or dead.' |
| *McCarthy*: | 'From what?' |
| *Gleeson*: | 'When I seen her lying there.' |
| *McCarthy*: | 'For all you knew she might only have fallen there?' |
| *Gleeson*: | 'It could happen.' |
| *McCarthy*: | 'Why didn't you think of that? Why did you come to the conclusion that she might be dead or sleeping?' |

| | |
|---|---|
| *Gleeson*: | 'Well, I didn't bother my head about it. I didn't bother about seeing her but I doubled back from the ditch on the spot.' |
| *McCarthy*: | 'But people of course used to cross the land according to yourself, your neighbours?' |
| *Gleeson*: | 'Yes.' |
| *McCarthy*: | 'Did it occur to you that it might be one of your neighbours' wives or daughters?' |
| *Gleeson*: | 'No, sir.' |
| *McCarthy*: | 'Why?' |
| *Gleeson*: | 'Well, I don't know.' |
| *Judge*: | 'You didn't know? Why didn't that occur to you? What did you not know?' |
| *Gleeson*: | 'I didn't know the person when I came to the ditch.' |

Gleeson was then asked if he saw a dog with a lame leg, or a sheep caught in the fence, would he leave it there? His answer was no. Judge Maguire adjourned the court until the following morning.

### DAY EIGHT

## *Tuesday, 25 February 1941*

The second day of the prosecution's cross-examination of Harry Gleeson continued as the first had ended, with questions about how much he could see when he looked over the gap in the ditch. He maintained that the dog on the woman's chest had obstructed his view of her head, accounting for his failure to identify Moll McCarthy, whose feet lay pointing in his direction.

There followed one of those moments that mean little when described in a dusty court transcript. Yet an observer[21] who was present throughout the trial said the effect on the jury was palpable. Prosecution counsel Joseph A. McCarthy was cross-examining Harry Gleeson about his uncle John Caesar's gun and ammunition, and the garda search for discarded cartridges on the farm after the body had been found. The point here is that when Caesar's gun was fired, the shot left the muzzle, but the heavy cardboard cartridge stayed trapped in the barrel. Some of the cartridges the gardaí found had been twisted before they were discarded.

*McCarthy*: 'And they [the gardaí] were looking for cartridges?'

*Gleeson*: 'I suppose they were. '

*McCarthy*: 'You had used some of those cartridges yourself?'

*Gleeson*: 'Yes, sir.'

*McCarthy*: 'And this gun you used – the cartridges used to get stuck in it?'

*Gleeson*: 'Yes, sir.'

*McCarthy*: 'How would you take them out?'

*Gleeson*: 'I had a little strong nail and I put it in the barrel and the cartridge would hop out.'

*McCarthy*: 'Well here is a cartridge – show us how you used to get a cartridge out.'

*Gleeson, demonstrating how he did it*: 'I'd put it [the nail] in the barrel and shake it and the cartridge would pop out. '

*McCarthy*: 'Are you left-handed with the gun?'

*Gleeson*: 'Yes.'

*McCarthy*:   'And you can twist the cartridge?'
*Gleeson*:    'I could if I went about it.'
*McCarthy*:   'You must have strong hands.'
*Gleeson*:    'I have.'
*McCarthy*:   'The strongest hands in the parish?'
*Gleeson*:    'I would not say that.'

McCarthy then showed Gleeson two cartridges, exhibits 1 and 12.

*McCarthy*:   'You know it has been sworn that they have been fired by the gun out of your house?'
*Gleeson*:    'Yes.'
*McCarthy*:   'Did you ever twist a cartridge after it had been fired?'
*Gleeson*:    'No, sir.'

Judge Martin Maguire asked Gleeson if he could twist a cartridge with his bare hands.

*Gleeson*:    'Yes, I think so.'
*Judge, indicating a cartridge:* 'Is that one like exhibit no. 12?'
*Gleeson*:    'Yes.'
*Judge*:      'Will you twist it like the other one? Stand up and let me see you how do it. Go on, try hard.'
*Gleeson*:    'I could hardly do the same with that.'
*McCarthy*:   'Could you twist it the same as exhibit no. 1?'
*Gleeson* took the cartridge and twisted it.
*McCarthy*:   'It is not every one who could do that.'
*Gleeson*:    'It is not.'

The jury had now seen how familiar Gleeson was with handling guns, seen the strength of his hands and seen him twisting the used cartridge. Moments earlier he had denied that facility. He had been cleverly trapped into making a liar of himself, and the jury must have realised the significance of the tableau that Joseph A. McCarthy – aided by Martin Maguire – had just contrived. Gleeson knew guns, and though there was no direct connection between him and exhibits 1 and 12, such a connection looked more likely. Harry Gleeson's defence was now in serious trouble.

When Gleeson had finished giving his evidence, three defence witnesses were called: the architect Patrick Munden, to underline that Gleeson may not have recognised Moll's body when he looked into the stubble field, and incidentally to remind the jury of the prosecution's bad faith in presenting an inaccurate scene-of-crime map; a doctor whose main purpose was to show that men who wear the same pair of trousers for a week often have semen stains on them without having had sex with a woman, a point earlier conceded by the state pathologist; and Michael Barron, a director of the Clonmel greyhound racing track, who said he was a friend of Gleeson, and gave evidence about his deafness, and also vouched for his good character.

This trial was nearly over, but it still had a few surprises. Gleeson's senior counsel, James Nolan-Whelan, presented his summation to the jury for one hour and twenty minutes. He said that his client was 'the most unfortunate man in the country'. He was an innocent man with as high a character as any member of the jury, yet he had been charged with murder. That came about because, in the course of his work, he found himself in the vicinity of a serious crime. Anyone might happen to be in the vicinity of a crime scene, and encounter considerable difficulty in proving his innocence.

Nolan-Whelan went on to say that, despite the most searching investigation, not one piece of evidence was found of Gleeson having immoral relations with Moll McCarthy. The only evidence to support this came from the lips of two of her children. Sergeant Reynolds had told the jury that John Caesar's gun had been cleaned since it was last fired, but Superintendent Stapleton, a ballistics expert, did not say that the gun had been fired in the two or three days before he examined it. In fact, the gun had not been fired for some considerable time.

The defence senior counsel then turned to Michael McCarthy's evidence that placed Gleeson within the field where Moll was found. He said the boy was mistaken and that Gleeson had been at the plainly visible gap between the dug-out field and the stubble field. Long before the question of this sighting had been mentioned, Gleeson had told the gardaí that, while in the dug-out field, he had seen the greyhound playing with an old bovine skull and had put him on a lead; the boy had said the dog was running loose. The gardaí had combed the dug-out field looking for cartridges and they never asked Gleeson about the bovine skull. This was because the truth of what Gleeson was telling had been corroborated by the prosecution's silence on this point, not by its evidence. Michael McCarthy had clearly lied in his evidence about the bag – he said he had originally got it from John Halpin – but Halpin, a respectable man with nothing to hide, had given evidence that he had never given a bag to Michael.

The evidence they had heard had not controverted one fact in Gleeson's lengthy statement to the police, Nolan-Whelan submitted. He did not think that Gleeson's failure to identify the body in the field at first sight would trouble the jury. The little black dog was lying on the body, and it would be very difficult for Gleeson to see the victim's head. In any case, why would he lie about this? Gleeson had nothing to gain by pretending that he did not recognise the body.

The medical evidence pointed to Moll McCarthy having died on the Thursday morning, not on the previous evening, as the prosecution had alleged. The doctors were agreed that the body temperature was inexplicable if Moll had been killed the previous night. The doctors also agreed that she had died within two to five hours of having her last meal. Where did she get that meal? Not with Harry Gleeson because he was proved to have been in Caesar's house on the Wednesday night. Where had she been? Dr O'Connor had given evidence that when he examined the body, her clothes were dry. Her sons Patrick and Michael gave evidence that the night was wet, so if she had lain out all night her clothes would have been wet. Nolan-Whelan gave no reason for the defence failure to call Anastasia Cooney as a witness. Nor did he account for the failure to call John and Bridget Caesar, who could have given evidence of Gleeson's movements. One might have expected the parish priest, Father O'Malley, to be called to say that Gleeson was a law-abiding citizen – which he was.

The two teachers from Knockgraffon school, whom defence solicitor John Timoney had earlier sought to call as witnesses, did not appear either.

Nolan-Whelan's address to the jury was not completed when the court adjourned for the day. For ease of reading, the summary above covers both days.[22]

### DAY NINE

## *Wednesday, 26 February 1941*

James Nolan-Whelan continued his summation of the defence's case for the first hour. Then, for the prosecution, George Murnaghan said that the evidence of Harry's guilt was coercive. Moll McCarthy had last been seen alive going towards the dug-out field. It was in the middle of the country (in open country, we might say today) and she must have been on her way to keep an appointment. The second shot was unquestionably fired at the scene where she was found, and the suggestion that the first had been fired elsewhere and the body moved was too far-fetched to merit consideration. He conceded that the evidence connecting Gleeson with the victim was circumstantial. The bag that Michael McCarthy said belonged to his mother was found on the Caesar farm, confirming the prosecution's contention that she had gone to meet Gleeson in the expectation that he would give her potatoes. Nothing could explain why Gleeson had not looked to see whose body was lying in the field. And did the jury really believe that he did not know where his uncle kept his gun cartridges, and, if not, why did he lie about it?

Then Judge Martin Maguire started his lengthy summing up. He told the jury that he would decide how the law applied, and advise them on the facts of the case, but it was for them to reject his interpretation of the facts if they thought he was wrong.

He then made an outrageous assertion about Moll McCarthy's actions following the last sighting of her by her son Michael at about 5.30 p.m. on Wednesday, 20 November, going across the fields in a north-easterly direction. 'Someone must have gone to meet that woman somewhere in the neighbourhood of the dug-out, must have gone there with a gun, must have loaded it and waited for the victim, if she were not already there, must have fired and fired again.'

Maguire had adopted as fact the prosecution case. This is bedrock fact, he told the jury. Never mind that the jury had heard confirmed evidence that the body was moved, that the victim's coat had been buttoned up after she had been shot, the judge decided that everything happened in the field. He had also deter-mined, without doubt, the time of death. Even the most cursory reading of the evidence suggests that Moll McCarthy could have been killed elsewhere and her body placed in the field, and there was no conclusive evidence to verify the time of her death, because the two doctors who examined the body had reached contradictory conclusions.

To underline the enormity of this leap, the judge immediately continued by saying, 'Now before putting to you the case for the prosecution ...' and went on to give a concise summary:

1. Harry Gleeson shot Moll McCarthy between 5.30 and 5.45 p.m. on Wednesday, 20 November 1940, at or near where the body was found.
2. Thomas Hennessy heard the shots.
3. Gleeson used John Caesar's gun and ammunition.
4. He left his victim there dead or dying and went to Caesar's house just after 6 p.m.
5. He disposed of the gun cartridges at that time.
6. It took him only five or six minutes to get home, because the crime scene was about 500 yards away from Caesar's farmhouse.
7. Gleeson behaved strangely for the rest of the evening, going out and returning, reading a newspaper and putting it down, and going to bed early while there was still a guest on the premises, chatting to the Caesars by the fireside.
8. He visited the crime scene early the next morning and was seen by Michael McCarthy.
9. His statement that he later 'discovered' the body by looking over the ditch into an adjoining field was a sham, deceiving nobody.
10. He went to report his discovery to the gardaí, seeking to divert suspicion from himself.
11. He knew the body would soon be found when her children went to look for their mother.
12. His subsequent conduct was consistent with his guilt.
13. His subsequent statements were intended to mislead the Garda Síochána.
14. His motive was to get rid of Moll McCarthy for ever.
15. Marks found on the used cartridge cases were consistent with being fired from John Caesar's gun.

16. The bloodstains on Gleeson's clothing occurred when he had committed the murder.
17. He had arranged the deceased's limbs and clothing.
18. All the above points to the inescapable conclusion that Gleeson murdered Moll McCarthy.

The court adjourned for lunch and, when it resumed, the judge began a detailed examination of the prosecution's case, witness by witness. It must have seemed very tedious to the jury, who had heard it all over the previous week and a half. At length, he defended Garda William Quinlan's presentation of the scene-of-crime map but finally concluded that it did not matter. The arguments about what Gleeson could or could not see when he got up on the ditch and saw the body lying in the stubble field were moot, because he had admitted that if he had wanted to know who it was who was lying there, he could have looked.

Turning to the older McCarthy boys, Maguire referred to them as 'little boys', totally dependent on their mother. Yet Patrick was fifteen and had a full-time job working on a neighbouring farm. Michael had given evidence in court on two previous occasions, when a man was charged with and found guilty of a sexual assault on his sister Mary.

Maguire then began to speak about the potato bag, which Michael said belonged to his mother, and asked why nobody from the Caesar family had given evidence about it being found on their farm.

Mrs Caesar then spoke up from the well of the court. 'Pardon me, sir, they [meaning herself and her husband] were not called.' The judge ordered that she be ejected from the court.

Maguire continued to examine the prosecution case in detail until he was interrupted again. Thomas Markey, a juror, had become ill. He appeared to have had a heart attack.

The judge, who was noticeably taken aback by this occurrence, adjourned until the following morning, observing that one more day would finish the trial.

### DAY TEN

## Thursday, 27 February 1941

The following morning Thomas Markey said he was well again, and Maguire continued his examination of what he described as the major evidence against Gleeson. He took each prosecution witness's testimony in turn. For example, in discussing Michael McCarthy's evidence, the judge's restatement of it is almost as long as the original, and he questions no part of it. In dealing with the conversation said to have taken place between Gleeson and the two McCarthy sons, the judge failed to mention to the jury that neither son had given evidence that it had indeed taken place. Earlier, the judge had registered the defence's protests over the admissibility of this evidence, saying he would put it right in his charge to the jury, but he did not.

Garda Vincent Scully's evidence of the morning when Gleeson appeared at the door of New Inn garda station to report finding a body gets the same near-verbatim retelling by the judge. Maguire can find no

fault in the prosecution case, not even the suggestion
that it could take Michael an hour to walk down the
road to Knockgraffon National School, nor that the
state pathologist gave a different account of what
Moll McCarthy was wearing to that given by her
children and other witnesses. However, witnesses
whose testimony did not support the prosecution case
got short shrift. Maguire homed in on Tommy Reid's
'slowness of speech and thought ... giving evidence
with some reluctance ... in a manner associated with
people working on the land'.

Not content with casting doubt on Reid's mental
capacity, Maguire then moved to reduce the man's
credibility further by dismissing his account of having
been mistreated in garda custody. Every garda who
gave evidence 'had conducted the investigation
with perfect fairness and propriety,' declared the
judge.[23] Yet Gleeson's alibi depended on Reid, and the
decision on whether to believe him or not was one for
the jury, not for the judge.

Judge Maguire then criticised MacBride and
Nolan-Whelan, deploring lawyers who 'took un-
bridled licence' to attack policemen in the course of
their duties. Not only was Maguire undermining
Gleeson's defence, he was prejudging Reid's case
for assault against two gardaí. Also strange was
his dismissal in his summing up of two matters he
had earlier raised: the missing firearms register,
and Sergeant Daly's visit to Moll McCarthy on the
afternoon of her disappearance.

Worse was Maguire's treatment of the defence's
suggestion that Moll had first been shot somewhere
else, then brought to the dug-out field. According to

Maguire, this was 'far-fetched'. Within the first fifteen minutes of his address, he had dismissed aspects of the defence case as if they were fantasy. Maguire's charge to the jury ran to 122 typed pages, but he did not get to the defence case until page 89. The fact that he dealt with the defence case in a peremptory way, unlike his earlier point-by-point examination of the prosecution case, was a clear indication to the jury of the judge's belief in Harry Gleeson's guilt.

Marcus Bourke pointed out that six or seven of the assumptions in Judge Maguire's account of the murder in the field at 5.30 or 5.45 p.m. on the Wednesday had been challenged either in direct evidence or in cross-examination. Bourke observed: 'Neither Dr O'Connor's evidence on the warmth of the body nor Dr McGrath's surprise at it were mentioned. Both support the Thursday morning theory.' Bourke accused the judge of misleading the jury in his account of Patrick McCarthy's evidence, failing to mention that Patrick had gone looking for his mother on the night she disappeared, 'confining himself to a bland or telescoped version of this event: it was clearly based on illegible or incomplete notes'. Patrick McCarthy said he gone into the stubble field late that night accompanied by his dog where – according to the prosecution – his mother's body was lying, but he did not see her, nor did the dog with him react to the presence of a body. He then went home and stayed up until 1 a.m. but she did not come home. This was a shocking omission in the judge's summing-up to the jury.

And what are we to make of Maguire's speculations about Gleeson's motives and behaviour? 'If he was associating with Moll McCarthy, he couldn't very well do it openly, and if he was the father of the child [the one who died after three weeks] he was not going to let the world know about it … if he was carrying on immorally with her, he was not going to post it on the highways and byways. They were thrown together, himself and this woman, and they had known each other for fifteen years.' Maguire continued: 'You may think that he thought of being finished with her [*sic*], he was in a difficult position, living there with his uncle and aunt, without any contract, any tenure.'

In fact, no evidence was placed before the court that Gleeson was the father of any of Moll's seven children. Superintendent O'Mahony was allowed to say that Michael McCarthy had said it about the last short-lived child, but Michael himself did not say it when giving evidence. What the judge had said in his charge to the jury was this: 'It was suggested that he [Gleeson] was the father of the last child, and there is evidence of the little boy [Michael McCarthy] that she [Mary McCarthy] definitely charged him [Gleeson] with being the father of the child [Peggy] and threatened to sue him.' Unsurprisingly, the appeal court later rebuked the judge for this gross misrepresentation of what had happened in this trial.

The judge's summing-up concluded with a series of rhetorical questions. Did Harry Gleeson have a motive for murdering Moll McCarthy? Did he have an opportunity to murder her? Did he have the means to do so? Judge Martin Maguire invited the jury to go away and answer these questions, having made it clear that he thought the answer to all three was yes. The time was just after 4 p.m.

We can only imagine the consternation on the defence bench as Maguire sent the jury to consider its verdict. So much of Maguire's summing up was partisan – the question was which aspect should Nolan-Whelan and MacBride target first? Nolan-Whelan made the best of a bad hand when he asked Judge Maguire in open court to recall the jury so that the judge could remind them that the sole evidence suggesting that Gleeson was the father of Mary McCarthy's child Peggy was one sentence that Michael McCarthy claimed to have overheard in an exchange between Gleeson and Mary McCarthy over her trespassing goats.

James Nolan-Whelan urged the judge to remind the jury that the conversation alleged to have taken place between Gleeson and Patrick and Michael McCarthy had not been put to them when they were in the witness box. He also complained that the judge had not noted that the two boys contradicted each other about their mother receiving potatoes from Gleeson. Patrick said he had never seen it happen. Nolan-Whelan also pointed out that the judge had told the jury that John Caesar's gun was kept in Gleeson's bedroom – the evidence was that it was kept in the bedroom shared by John and Bridget Caesar.

Maguire replied that Nolan-Whelan had made those points several times to the jury. As judge, he had told the jury to pay attention to everything counsel had said. He could not be expected to repeat every word said by counsel, prosecution or defence.

Nolan-Whelan countered that these matters were vital to the defence case, and said that the judge's summing-up had been lopsided. He also asked the judge to remind the jury that although the Wednesday night had been wet, on Thursday morning Dr O'Connor had noticed that Mary McCarthy's clothing was dry.

The judge replied that this point had been made repeatedly by the defence, but he did recall the jury at 4.25 p.m. and directed them on what he said were 'one or two points'. He admitted being wrong in saying that John Caesar's shotgun was kept in Gleeson's bedroom. He had also erred in saying that Patrick McCarthy had said he had seen Gleeson giving potatoes to his mother.

However, Judge Maguire's 'clarification' of his summary of the evidence about Gleeson's exchange with the McCarthy brothers did the defence no favours. He admits there was no direct evidence of that exchange. However: 'The account is given by the superintendent [O'Mahony] who says he can give it [accurately] because he made a note of it at the time', according to the judge.

The court record tells us what happened next:

> The jury again retired at 4.32 p.m. and returned at 6.29 p.m. with the finding that Gleeson is guilty with a strong recommendation for mercy. When asked if he had anything to say as to why the sentence of death should not be awarded against him, the accused replied: 'I had neither hand, act nor part in it.'
>
> His lordship [Judge Martin Maguire] thereupon pronounced sentence of death, the execution being fixed for March 24th, 1941. To the jury, the judge said: 'I think it is right that

I should say that I agree with your verdict, gentlemen. The recommendation that you made will be submitted immediately to the proper authorities.'

The jury had taken little under two hours to reach its verdict. James Nolan-Whelan immediately sought permission to appeal on the grounds of the judge's constant interruption of the witnesses' evidence, which he said showed bias, and his misdirection of the jury.

The judge refused the application.

The surprise here is the rider to the jury's verdict. How can twelve men convict a man of a foul and brutal murder and in the same breath enter a strong plea for mercy? It is tempting to speculate that the recommendation for mercy was linked with the sudden 'illness' and recovery of the juror Thomas Markey. Did he challenge the majority view? Did he threaten to withhold support for the guilty verdict? Was the recommendation for mercy the price of his assent? There is no knowing. The secrets of that jury room have never been revealed.

A garda who was in court on that fateful day said that he was struck by the way in which Gleeson responded to the guilty verdict. He repeated the words he had used in the earlier hearing in Clonmel. 'I had neither hand, act nor part in it', in the same firm tone.[24]

A friend of Gleeson's spoke briefly to him as he was taken away to Mountjoy Jail, and then met the Caesars, Bridget and John, returning to the courtroom, their eyes full of tears.

Part of the guilty verdict document signed by the foreman of the jury Joseph Fahy, showing the 'strong recommendation to mercy'. COURTESY NATIONAL ARCHIVES.

But the day's work was not yet over for Martin Maguire. Before he could go home to his house in the Dublin suburb of Clonskeagh, he had one final task to carry out. Back in his chambers, he sat down at his desk, took out his fountain pen and wrote a note and personally addressed it to the Minister for Justice, Gerry Boland.

> I beg to inform you that the trial concluded this day of Henry Gleeson, convicted of the murder of Mary McCarthy at Marlhill, Co Tipperary. The jury found the prisoner guilty <u>with a strong recommendation to mercy.</u> [The underlining was clearly done at the time of writing. The broad nib strokes confirm that.] I sentenced the prisoner to death – the execution to take place on 24 March 1941.

Martin Maguire then put on his hat and coat and went home.

# 4. Moll's Last Hours Reconsidered

Before leaving the guilty verdict, we should look more closely at the deposition of the state pathologist, Dr John McGrath, which was lodged in court before the first hearing. It is possible to read it in a very different light from that adopted at the trial. At the Dublin trial, the focus was on vain attempts to reconcile the conflicting findings of the two doctors – Dr O'Connor and Dr McGrath – over the time of death. Put that aside, and another picture emerges.

Dr O'Connor had made the first examination. He described seeing the body lying in the field, finding that the victim's clothing was dry, rigor mortis was complete and the body temperature was 96 degrees Fahrenheit, or three degrees below the normal living reading. 'I placed my hand on the body under the clothes and formed the impression that it was warmer than it should have been in the condition of the weather. I am not in a position to say whether the warmth I noticed could have been caused by a dog lying on it [the body].' The following day, Dr O'Connor assisted the state pathologist to carry out a post-mortem examination.

The body of Moll McCarthy in the stubble field. COURTESY NATIONAL ARCHIVES

What was missed at the trial, I suggest, was that Dr McGrath's detailed examination of the body permitted a very different account of the last hours of Moll McCarthy's life from that put forward by the prosecution, and indeed by the defence. The following is based on his deposition.

Dr McGrath arrived at New Inn at about 10.15 a.m. on Friday, 22 November. Moll McCarthy's body been lying in the field for at least twenty-four hours at that stage, covered first by a sheet and then a police tarpaulin since the previous day. 'The body lay near a fence towards the corner of a partly ploughed field.' It lay near a place where 'persons had frequently gone over the fence'. 'The body was lying on its back ... the body was fully clothed.' There were three pieces of bone on the ground close to the head, and a cartridge wad nearby.

The state pathologist went on to say that the clothes were not disarranged, and they had various bloodstains on them. 'The condition of the clothes indicated that the body had been moved after it had fallen ... consistent with a person having lifted the legs and moved them away from the fence, assuming the body had fallen in the place where it was found with its legs towards the fence.'

Dr McGrath said that he found no signs of a struggle adjacent to the body. He then asked that the body be taken to New Inn garda station. 'There were two cartridge wads under the head.' There was some moist blood on the ground under and to the left of the head. The sod of earth where the head had lain was removed and examined a fortnight later. One might wonder why this delay? What use could the sod be so long after the event?

'There was an area rather bare of grass under the head.' Where the body lay 'the grass and stone looked and felt dry'. Curiously, Dr McGrath's account had not yet mentioned that the unfortunate victim's face was gone.

At New Inn, McGrath began to perform a post-mortem examination, assisted by Dr O'Connor.

The deceased was wearing a tweed coat and skirt and brown stockings, and mismatched shoes. 'There were bloodstains here and there on the outside of the coat.' The coat was buttoned up when the body was found. Nevertheless, bloodstains were found inside the coat on both the left- and right-hand sides of the body. There were also pieces of tissue stuck to the blood on the inner left-hand side of the coat. These stains showed no corresponding stains on the pullover beneath the coat. There were bloodstains on the outside of the skirt in front, some under the coat, others on the inside upper band of the skirt.

So there were bloodstains on the outside of the victim's coat without matching stains on the garments she had been wearing under the coat.

The state pathologist went on to describe bloodstains around the collar and left shoulder, of the kind you would expect to find in a person who was killed by a shot to the head or neck. Under her coat, she was wearing a white pullover pulled up to the line of her nipples, showing bloodstains, as one might expect.

Then we come to the skirt. This is the skirt of a woman shot twice in the head, and she is wearing a fully buttoned-up coat. 'The skirt had fasteners on the left side. Three were open but the skirt was fastened at the waist with a safety pin. Under the skirt was a slip, which was blood-stained on the front of the waist. Under this was a corset which showed practically no blood signs.' Below the corset, she was wearing an undervest, predictably stained with blood at the neck area, and a piece of her lip and a small piece of bone were lodged there. Under the white slip she wore blue knickers properly arranged, with some bloodstains, also on the skin in that area. 'In the body rigor mortis was well present' and there was some dried blood on her hands.

Before we pass on to Dr McGrath's examination of Moll McCarthy's wounds, it is worth considering what he has already told us. If someone wearing a fully buttoned up overcoat is shot twice with a shotgun, you expect there to be bloodstains on the outer clothing, apart from the neck and shoulder area where there might be an open collar and blood seeps down and stains accordingly. Blood would also spatter on the coat and seep into the garments inside it, particularly if the first shot was fired when the victim was standing up, as the prosecution alleged had been the case. That clearly is not what happened to Moll McCarthy. Someone clearly had buttoned up her coat *after* she was dead.

Dr McGrath found pellet marks on the left shoulder below the murdered woman's ear. 'The pellets had come from a point almost directly to left [*sic*] and about the same height as left shoulder.' So Moll McCarthy was shot standing up. 'In the centre of the pellet marks there were a ragged hole into the neck. This was about ¾ inch in diameter. The main mass of pellets had penetrated through this hole … [had] torn and damaged the neck tissue … punctured the internal carotid artery and jugular vein and struck the spine and fractured it.' Dr McGrath went on to describe other less serious wounds, noting the absence of blood in their vicinity, or indeed elsewhere about the body. And he noted that there were traces of a recent meal in the victim's stomach.

The state pathologist's finding can be read as supporting the case that Moll McCarthy was killed somewhere other than the stubble field and that she was not wearing some or all those clothes when she died, and was then dressed and taken to the spot where her body was eventually discovered.

Then there is the question of her blood. Where did it go? Even Judge Martin Maguire remarked on this. Moll would have had eight pints of blood in her when she was shot. If she had lived for a while after she had been shot, her heart would have pumped blood out through the wound. If she had died straightaway, as Dr McGrath thought likely, there would be a loss of blood through the wound, but it would not gush out, because the heart would have stopped pumping.

The pattern of bloodstains on Moll McCarthy's clothing simply does not support the prosecution's theory that she was shot once while standing up in the stubble field, with the second shot being fired at her where she lay, having fallen to the ground. A more credible scenario has one shot fired at her and killing her in another place, after which her body was brought to the field where it was found. There, a second shot was fired, taking away her face.

But why a second shot, if she was dead already? The idea put forward by the prosecution that it was to conceal her identity does not stand up. She lived less than a mile from where she was found. Her children passed through the Caesars' fields many times a day. There would be no difficulty in identifying Moll McCarthy by her clothes.

Another theory floated at the time – though it was not mentioned in court – is that the person who fired the second shot hated women. This has to be considered, given Moll's particular way of life. The killing of prostitutes – and it should be said that in the course of the trial Mary McCarthy was never described thus – is often linked to a hatred of women. If that were the case, one would expect other similar murders to follow, but there were none – and Moll was not the only woman of her kind in the neighbourhood.

The greatest likelihood is that Moll McCarthy had a rendezvous with a man or men in the disused Lynch farmhouse nearby. That may account for the evidence that she had had sex not long before she was killed. The medical examination evidence suggested consensual sex. We have to consider that she could have been beaten and the shot removing her face could have removed evidence of that.

Was there a row?

Was Moll's assailant concerned about the possibility that she was having sex with Sergeant Anthony Daly and that she might have said something to him about the current activities of neighbours who were former IRA men? Daly had called to her cottage on that Wednesday afternoon, Garda Ruth had done the same two days earlier. Did a man strike her in the face before she had put on her coat, and even perhaps her skirt? Others were involved – they had to be so the body could be moved. Someone had to dress her and button up her coat, and help carry her body from where she was killed to where she was found. Did her assailant summon these others after the event or were they present before she was shot? Was this some kind of interrogation and punishment beating that went too far? The shot that took away Moll's face also took away any evidence that might have pointed to a previous injury to the head and neck.

The most likely course of events is that, after Moll was killed in Lynch's disused farmhouse or similar hiding place, her body lay there for some hours and, before dawn, two or three people, almost certainly men, shifted it to the stubble field, where Harry Gleeson came across it on Thursday morning when he went out to check on his uncle's livestock. Some of those men, I believe, had been at a meeting of the members of the Local Security Force in Cahir the previous evening, at which Thomas Hennessy, who combined running a local shebeen (he sold cider which he probably made with his own apples) with being second in command of the New Inn B group of the Local Security Force – providing back-up for the Garda Síochána – was present, and at which Superintendent Patrick O'Mahony was represented, if he was not there in person.

# 5. Appeal

When news of the jury's verdict, including the recommendation for mercy, arrived in the Department of Justice, wheels began to turn. A very senior official in the Taoiseach's office, Pádraig Ó Cinnéide,[1] wrote to the Garda Commissioner requesting 'that a report be furnished immediately as to the facts of the case and the previous career, character and circumstances of the prisoner'. This request was passed down the line to Superintendent Patrick O'Mahony in Cahir who – as we shall see – took it as an invitation to justify himself. A more likely purpose for the Ó Cinnéide request was to find out why the jury made a recommendation for mercy for a man it had just convicted of a very brutal crime, and if there were any grounds for acting on that recommendation.

On the same day, solicitor John Timoney lodged an appeal against the death sentence imposed on his client. This had the effect of putting off the hanging until the appeal had been heard and judgment given. The main point of appeal was that Judge Martin Maguire's charge to the jury was 'incomplete, defective, unsatisfactory and incorrect' and it listed twenty-seven specific points of the defence case affected. The date for the hearing of the appeal was set for 31 March 1941.

The defence team then set about putting together its case. Back in New Inn, John Timoney's efforts focused on what he had learned from Anastasia Cooney's statement to him, made just before Gleeson's trial had begun. She was staying with her brother-in-law, District Justice Rice, in the Dublin suburb of Rathgar for the duration of the trial and when visiting Harry Gleeson in Mountjoy Jail after his conviction. She gave a statement in which she said that she had once asked Moll McCarthy who the father of her last child (Peggy) was, but Moll insisted that she would not divulge the name because she had promised the father that she would not do so. Miss Cooney's statement said that she thought the father was a man called McKay or McKee, an unemployed man with a large family who lived not far away on the Shanbally road with people called Devitt. She knew he had called frequently to Moll's cottage, and that Moll met him sometimes in Cashel. This was well known in the neighbourhood and must have been known to the police, she said. The McKay family had stayed at Moll's cottage some years earlier but had left when a dispute arose between McKay's wife and Moll.

Knowing this, Anastasia Cooney had asked Moll if Peggy's father was a married man. Moll, she said, had understood this to be a reference to McKay, and replied: 'There was no harm in it – there was nothing like that in it.' She took this to be a denial that McKay had fathered the child. However, she also told John Timoney that she could not always rely on Moll to tell the truth. Miss Cooney also mentioned a man called Jenkins of Knockgraffon who was reputed to be the father of another of Moll's children. His name was not on the list Harry Gleeson had given to the police the day after he found the body. 'She also mentioned Burns in that context.' said Anastasia Cooney. (This is Patrick Byrne, the father of Patrick McCarthy, Moll's eldest son.)

Anastasia Cooney insisted that Harry Gleeson's name had never come up in connection with Moll McCarthy and that Moll had never mentioned him to her. She – Anastasia Cooney – had never heard anything bad said against Gleeson.

A sergeant by the name of Doyle knew Moll very well and was often in her cottage, according to Anastasia Cooney.[2]

A traveller's wife by the name of O'Reilly had attended Moll for Peggy's birth. Some weeks after the birth, the infant became unwell and Moll had sent for Miss Cooney, who could not go to her that night. When she arrived the following morning, the baby was dead. The child, although not deformed, might have been premature, Anastasia Cooney thought. Her head was very large in relation to her body, she said. There were gypsies or travelling people at the cottage then. Moll asked if she might bury the child in a burial place belonging to the Cooney family. The travellers produced a small box they had made to serve as the baby's coffin. Miss Cooney agreed to this. So far as she knew, the McCarthys dug the grave and there were no burial expenses. She thought that two New Inn gardaí, Joseph Ruth and Vincent Scully, had seen the body prior to burial, but did not say why.

Anastasia Cooney said she had 'stood for' (acted as godparent to) several of Moll's children and had intervened to see that the last child was christened.

In the months before her brutal death, Moll had asked Anastasia Cooney to help her try to get a house somewhere else. The cottage had become too dilapidated for her and her children to live in. Moll had agreed to approach the local medical officer of health to see if the cottage could be condemned as unfit for human habitation. However, Miss Cooney later learned that Moll had never done this.

Over the years, Moll had let Miss Cooney know that she received financial or other support from the various fathers of her brood. According to Cooney, Michael was the brightest, and a little girl younger than him was also very intelligent. (This was either Nellie or Bridget.) Mary McCarthy, the eldest, might be worth talking to, Miss Cooney told John Timoney, but she was 'very slow and hard to obtain any information from'. She said she had seen the children once since their mother had died, and had started to question them, but they had begun to cry, so she had desisted. Anastasia Cooney finished by saying that she would prefer not to be called to give evidence at the Court of Criminal Appeal, but would do so if it became necessary.

After Gleeson was convicted, Anastasia Cooney wrote to the Minister for Justice, Gerry Boland. The letter is undated but there are identical copies in the MacBride and Bourke files. In her letter, she told the minister that she had spoken to the children in the county home. 'Michael and Mary, who both gave evidence at the trial, told me that during the night of the 20th November, their brother Patrick went with a lantern into the field where Mary McCarthy's body was found, and went over to the actual spot it was found, but that her body was not there then. This would have been sometime after 11 p.m.' She went on to say that her information was based on her conversation with Mary and Michael, because Patrick was at work on the day she had spoken to his siblings.

On 21 February 1941, while Gleeson's trial in Dublin was under way, Timoney received a note from Thomas Gleeson, a nephew of Harry, which contained the following information: 'There is a man in the village of New Inn, a tailor Joseph Moloney, who states he heard two shots on the morning of the death of Mary McCarthy. He told the P.P. [parish priest, Father O'Malley] who told him to tell the Gardaí. He did not do so. The public knows this.'

Timoney's note recorded what then happened. 'I visited Joseph Moloney on Saturday, 22 March 1941. He confirmed the matters set out in the paragraph above, and also informed me that Patrick Coman of Lough Kent East, New Inn, had also told him he had heard the two shots on the morning of Thursday, 21 November.'

Moloney was a retired tailor and his son also worked as a tailor at Rockwell College, about a mile from Marlhill, but he had recently enlisted in the British army, so his father came out of retirement to fill in for him. There are two strands to Moloney's new evidence. The first is Moloney's own account of going to work on foot from his home at Lough Kent East, New Inn, on the Thursday morning when the body was found. He remembered the Clonmel bus passing his house as he ate his breakfast, so the time was then about 9.10 a.m. A little later, he saw Father O'Malley on his way to say 9.30 a.m. Mass. Soon after passing through the village, Moloney heard two shots, in quick succession. They came from the direction of John Caesar's farm. He said he had owned a double-barrelled shotgun years earlier, and knew the way 'you shifted your finger from one trigger to another and taking quick aim again'. The New Inn church bell for morning Mass was ringing as he heard the shots, so it was 9.25 a.m., just minutes before Harry Gleeson said he had found the body. Moloney said he had told Pat Coman, who had said he had also heard the shots. Moloney said that when he found out that Moll McCarthy's clothes were dry, he knew that the shots he had heard that morning were the ones that had killed her. Here Moloney has offered yet another version of the events surrounding the death of Moll McCarthy.

Joseph Moloney had gone to Father O'Malley, who had advised him to tell the gardaí. 'I told him I would not.' Later, when Harry Gleeson was being sent for trial, Moloney said Father O'Malley told him not to bother about it, because the gardaí knew that Moll McCarthy had died on the Wednesday night.

Timoney's note continued:

> He [Moloney] also told me that he had heard that a man whose name he believed to be either Fitzgerald or Fitzpatrick had fired two shots at a cat on the evening of Wednesday November 21st, 1940; that he [Moloney] had discussed this matter with Guard Scully of New Inn who had told him that Sergeant Anthony Daly had

interviewed the man who shot the cat but only one bullet had been fired at the cat. Moloney added that a man named Mike Gorman of New Inn would be able to tell who shot the cat.

Timoney said he then visited Mike Gorman and Patrick Coman, both of whom lived around New Inn. Coman confirmed that he too had heard two shots in quick succession, as Moloney had said. Gorman told him that he was probably looking for John Fitzgerald of Knockgraffon. 'I went to the house of John Fitzgerald and interviewed him. He told me that about dusk on the evening of [Wednesday] November 20, 1940, he fired a shot at a cat.'

On Tuesday, 25 March 1941, Timoney got a signed statement from John Fitzgerald. He also got a signed statement from Patrick Coman of Lough Kent East, and filed copies of both in the office of the court registrar in Dublin. In the meantime, he met Michael Long, an employee of Fitzgerald, who said he 'remembered well a cat having been shot by John Fitzgerald ... on the evening that Moll McCarthy was shot'. He also said that two shots were fired at the cat.

Timoney had done well. This new evidence would put Harry Gleeson in the clear on Wednesday around 6 p.m. by accounting for the shots that Hennessy said he had heard. The notion that Gleeson had shot Moll McCarthy twice, moved the body, rushed home, changed his bloodstained clothes, washed himself, and sat down for his tea in the Caesars' farmhouse in the space of fifteen minutes was always nonsense anyway. Add to that Moloney's account of hearing shots on the Thursday morning, and the prosecution case for Moll McCarthy having been killed the previous evening should have been in tatters.

However, between making his statement and signing it, Michael Long retracted his earlier statement, insisting that only one shot was fired on the Wednesday evening. The cat had been in a tree and when it fell to the ground after being shot, a fellow workman, Edmond Barrett, had finished it off with a stick. Timoney then contacted Edmond Barrett, who first said there were two shots, then corrected himself, saying that John Fitzgerald had fired the second shot at the cat the next day.

So Fitzgerald had fired a shot at a cat in a tree on the Wednesday night, Barrett had finished it off with a stick, and Fitzgerald had shot it again the next day. Somebody was telling lies, and the net effect of them was to remove an innocent explanation for the shots Thomas Hennessy said he had heard on the Wednesday evening and which the jury believed Harry Gleeson had shot dead Moll McCarthy. Thus one promising lead for the appeal had appeared and just as quickly had been closed off.

The question is: who had got at the witnesses?

John Timoney and Seán MacBride had met Father O'Malley before the trial. They asked the New Inn parish priest to give a character reference for Harry Gleeson. He declined, but added that Anastasia Cooney thought well of him. He also told Timoney what he knew about Tommy Reid being beaten up in the barracks, and of Reid's eye being discoloured when he saw him the next day.

On 25 March, Timoney went again to the parish priest. Time was running out and the likelihood of

Gleeson going to the gallows was increasing daily. He asked Father O'Malley to confirm to him what the tailor Joseph Moloney had told him about hearing shots on the Thursday morning. The priest did so, and said he found Moloney to be a truthful man, but again he refused to sign a statement.

Below in full is Timoney's draft of the statement the priest agreed was correct but refused to sign:

> I am here [in New Inn] for the last eight and a half years. I came here on 23/4/1932. Harry's pedigree is not good. The parents of his neighbour's children used to tell their children to keep away from Harry when he was going to school.
>
> His family generally are not up to much. He would be capable of doing queer things – in the line of taking things belonging to others and hiding them – not exactly [*sic*].
>
> Moll McCarthy told me the names of the fathers of all the children except the last. From the time that I came here to New Inn to the birth of the Mahony child [Bridget, whose father was a cook at Rockwell College], Moll was very good and used attend the First Friday etc. After that she fell out with me: but about two years ago after my operation Moll made friends with me – having welcomed me home – but I never went near her since.
>
> Miss Cooney of Garranlea [president of the local branch of the Legion of Mary] acted as a go-between, and used to tell me everything she'd hear since I fell out with Moll after the

O'Mahony child. Neither Miss Cooney nor I ever heard of the paternity of the last child.

I think that neither Mary nor Patrick (Moll's oldest children) would look unfavourably on Moll's having (more) children.

I tried twice to get the children committed [to an orphanage] – the last time about two years ago. At that time, one was guilty of stealing, and 'twas brought on [prosecuted] by the guards. The other child had become incorrigible about going to school. District Justice Troy would not commit them, and I believe it was poverty brought her so bad in recent times as she had such a lot of mouths to feed out of the small state relief she was getting.

I was never told that Harry Gleeson was the father of the last child. If the neighbours knew it, they wouldn't tell me because I was very friendly with Mrs Caesar, and used often call to the Caesars, and get Mass offerings from Mrs Caesar.

So according to Father O'Malley, Harry Gleeson was a bad boy when he was at school and nothing much had changed since. The McCarthy children were thieves, did not go to school and should be locked up in an orphanage. Nor did the older ones care how many more illegitimate children their mother had. Mrs Caesar was a good woman who gave him money for Masses.

Father O'Malley was known to place great importance on money. A woman from the nearby townland of Boytonrath said in 2012 that she recalled his stooped figure in a black soutane, tinged green with age, standing guard over the collection plate at Sunday mass to make sure everyone put in their fair share.[3] O'Malley, who professed to be a friend of Bridget Caesar, proved more ready to bury Caesar's nephew than to do anything to save him from the gallows.

Around the same time, Father Denis Blackburn, the curate called to administer the last rites when the body was found, told Timoney: 'I don't want to have anything to do with giving evidence in this case.' With spiritual shepherds so lacking in moral compass, is it any wonder that the flock in New Inn went astray?

Harry Gleeson's appeal was heard in the Court of Criminal Appeal over four days: 31 March to 3 April 1941. Three judges heard the case: the chief justice, Timothy Sullivan, and two judges from the High Court, Conor Maguire and Henry Hanna. Such appeals are limited in scope, being based on the transcript of the case being appealed and any new evidence the court permits the defence to offer. The words prosecution and defence are used here in the way they were in the criminal trial.

The first two days consisted of Nolan-Whelan listing the flaws in Judge Martin Maguire's presentation to the jury, in particular, Maguire's failure to mention that Moll's clothes were found to be dry, despite the prosecution case that she had lain out all night in wet weather. MacBride then dealt with how the new evidence made the guilty verdict unreliable.

The prosecution too deployed the same team as before. Joseph A. McCarthy suggested that Moll McCarthy's clothes dried out overnight (on a wet

November night). George Murnaghan suggested that a sheet placed over the body might have kept her clothes dry. The only real difficulty the prosecution side encountered was when Joseph A. McCarthy began to suggest that Harry Gleeson was the father of the seventh child. He backed off quickly when the judges expressed displeasure at him making a suggestion that had not been proved at the trial, even though Judge Martin Maguire had, in fact, managed to drag it in.

Chief Justice Sullivan queried McCarthy on the bullets used, appearing to suggest that Harry Gleeson should not have been convicted unless the bullets used had been produced and connected to him. Judge Hanna was the only criminal lawyer on the bench and his interventions tended to favour the prosecution side. He defended the prosecution decision not to call John and Bridget Caesar as witnesses. Hanna homed in on the conversation between Gleeson and the two older McCarthy boys, saying that the defence could have recalled them to question them. Hanna noted that he could not understand Gleeson's hazy memory of that conversation.

The official record of the appeal is sparse and, as was customary, did not contain details of the submissions made. The *Tipperary Star* had a reporter in court, and what we know is owed to him, and to some notes in lawyers' files, including a rough handwritten note probably made by the chief justice, which was included in the National Archives' file on the main trial when I first inspected it.

The judgment refusing the appeal was short. Every judge had his own way of summing up a case for the jury, the appeal court held. The handwritten notes made by one of the appeal judges set it out thus:

> This court cannot lay down either as a matter of law or of practice that a judge should charge a jury in a particular manner so long as he puts the case for the defence to the jury.

Judge Maguire's omission of Moll's dry clothing from his charge to the jury was not serious enough to warrant quashing the conviction. Superintendent O'Mahony's evidence about the conversation involving Moll's sons was not ideal – 'it would have been more proper to examine the McCarthys [Patrick and Michael] about the [disputed] conversation' – but this did not make the evidence inadmissible.

The new evidence produced also fell short of their lordships' exacting requirements. Neither Harry Gleeson nor Tommy Reid had spoken of hearing shots on the Thursday morning. The new evidence was inconsistent with that already given, and 'no reasonable jury should be influenced by the evidence of Moloney and Coman'. Underlying this was the understandable suspicion that the Moloney/Coman account of hearing shots on Thursday morning was just too convenient a way of muddying the waters of Gleeson's conviction to be credible at this late stage.

So the appeal was lost.

Marcus Bourke noted that the Court of Criminal Appeal judgment completely ignored the ballistics evidence.[4] Bill O'Connor's overall summation of the trial maintained that nobody had ever understood the ballistics evidence, and what it was supposed to prove.[5] The appeal court appeared to have got there before him, yet it took up two days of the trial.

One can only wonder if the learned judges were ever troubled in later life by the thought that they had been given an opportunity to remedy a great wrong and had failed to grasp it.

There now remained the possibility of an appeal to the Supreme Court. For that to happen the defence was required to seek leave to appeal. On 15 April, eight days before Gleeson was due to hang, Timoney wrote to the Attorney General, Kevin Haugh SC, enclosing a memorandum drafted by Nolan-Whelan and MacBride, listing twenty-five matters in Maguire's charge to the jury which they said were defective. Within twenty-four hours Haugh had refused the certificate.

In the meantime, MacBride wrote privately to the Minister for Justice, Gerry Boland, on Good Friday, 11 April, enclosing documents challenging the guilty verdict. While all this was going on in Dublin, matters were proceeding on a different tack in County Tipperary. In early March, Superintendent Patrick O'Mahony was clearly coming under pressure to justify Harry Gleeson's conviction. The verdict of twelve good men and true had not been enough. Taoiseach Éamon de Valera had received expressions of concern over the verdict and sentence via his friend Michael Ryan, a Triple Crown winning rugby international from Cashel.

In fact, more than that had happened behind the scenes. People in Cahir and New Inn had noticed that the case was being reinvestigated, and that Sergeant Anthony Daly was not in the loop.

According to Marcus Bourke: 'Plain-clothes men from Dublin came and went and it was observed that most of those questioned were friends of Sergeant Daly.' Local people were openly speculating that Moll McCarthy's body had *not* lain out overnight in the stubble field. Rumours were now spreading openly in the parish of New Inn that Anthony Daly had either been 'tipped off' in advance about the murder and had failed to prevent it, or had actively connived in bringing it about. He was either a bad policeman or an ineffectual one. Father O'Malley found it necessary to preach a sermon warning of the dangers of mischievous speculation, in which he defended Daly. The sergeant was in for a rough time for his remaining seven years in New Inn until his retirement.

Patrick O'Mahony got wind of this and issued threats or warnings to local people not to cooperate with the reinvestigation. In response to the request received from the Department of Justice via the garda commissioner, he prepared a document headed 'Murder – Mary McCarthy', dated 3 March 1941, setting out his case against Harry Gleeson, and which was much more damning than the case the prosecution had made out in court.

After sketching out the background, O'Mahony set about doing two things in this document: he began with a summary of the prosecution case against Gleeson, along with a sympathetic account of Moll McCarthy's struggle to feed and clothe her growing brood; he then bolstered his case against Gleeson with material not given in evidence at the trial. In doing so, he gratuitously impugned the reputation of the wider Gleeson family without any proof.

According to O'Mahony, a neighbour's servant thirty years earlier had accused Thomas Gleeson, Harry's father, of fathering an illegitimate child. The mother had left the child on Thomas Gleeson's doorstep. He had thrown the infant into a clump of briars from where a neighbour had rescued it.

'Two of Henry Gleeson's brothers were accused of being the fathers of illegitimate children. When one of these occurrences took place, Henry got a bad beating from the brothers of the girl concerned because he prevented a marriage between the boy and the girl.'

Harry's mother was a well-known shoplifter, according to O'Mahony, as were two of her sons – though none of the three was ever prosecuted. This, of course, was hearsay, given without any proof and no justification, and is included here only to show the lengths to which O'Mahony was prepared to go in his pursuit of Harry Gleeson.

Turning to more recent matters, O'Mahony claimed that John Caesar had told the gardaí that he would throw out his nephew if he were associating with Moll. 'It is known that the deceased [Moll McCarthy] was issuing some sort of threat to Gleeson. The fact that his uncle might find out the true position would be sufficient motive for the crime. He had arrived at the time when it was either a life of comparative ease and security for him on his uncle's land or the life of a homeless labourer. He had to silence his accuser.'

> That Gleeson is the type of man capable of committing this crime, there is no doubt. He is possibly something of a sadist. He admits opening a knife to young McCarthy ... on 15

August 1934, he fired two shots at a number of young boys with whom he had been hurling an hour or so earlier. Pellets struck two of them. In 1939, a shot was fired at a young man who passed by Caesar's yard. He was struck by pellets in the back. The next day he challenged Caesar and Gleeson over it. They just laughed at him.

O'Mahony added that the shooting incidents were hushed up, and that Gleeson was never reported to the gardaí for anything more than drinking 'after hours'.

The document concludes with O'Mahony's assessment of the man he had accused of murder.

In manner, he was glum and distant. He mixed very little with the general public. Although usually calm and self-possessed, he was cunningly cruel when his temper was roused. He was not known to mix much with members of the female sex. His name was linked with that of a neighbouring farmer's daughter a few years ago. The association, if any, was very little and had faded out long ago.

There is no trace of insanity in any branch of Gleeson's family ... the father's immoral tendencies and the mother's thieving instincts seem to have been fairly well transmitted to the children. If his uncle's intentions towards him were not taken into consideration, he should be regarded as penniless.

A policeman is expected to be able to justify actions taken in the course of an investigation, but this document, laced with bad-minded gossip and unproven and improbable assertions about people with no clear link to the case, goes much further than that. Patrick O'Mahony was clearly looking to silence critics of his conduct of the murder inquiry. He would die in 1980 without having done so. The interesting thing is the timing – within a week of the guilty verdict, the conviction was in danger of unravelling. We do know that a copy of O'Mahony's mischief-making document went to the Department of Justice and was forwarded to the Department of the Taoiseach in April 1941 for circulation to the government (cabinet), prior to a final decision on execution. It was then withdrawn.

Back on the ground in County Tipperary, with Gleeson's execution fast approaching, John Timoney hastily arranged a petition asking the government 'to commute the sentence of death' passed on Henry Gleeson. A Tim Vokes, with an address in Summerhill, Dublin, wrote to MacBride asking for the names and addresses of the jurors, seeking their signatures for the petition, but we do not know what became of that. A carpenter named Martin Vokes had briefly given evidence at the trial of working at Caesar's farm in 1940 and borrowing a single-barrelled shotgun, and of seeing Harry Gleeson take it out. He was Harry Gleeson's nephew and lived in Galbertstown, near Holycross, Harry's home place, and was John Caesar's grandnephew, so it is safe to see in this evidence of family involvement in the petition to save Harry Gleeson from the gallows.

## PETITION FOR REPRIEVE OF HENRY GLEESON

WE, the undersigned, hereby humbly request the Government, pursuant to the provisions of the Constitution of Ireland, to advise the President to commute the sentence of death passed upon Henry Gleeson in the Central Criminal Court on the 27th day of March, 1941.

| NAME | ADDRESS |
|---|---|
| Mary Mason | Bally-vera Ardfinnan |
| Alice Ryan | Patricks. Well. |
| Kathrine Bourke | Bally-vera. Ardfinnan. |
| Annie Quyer | Kulnockrin Rd Fethard |
| John Quyer | Kulnockrin Rd |
| Mary Maher | Main St Killenaule |
| M. G. Seagham | Main St. Tilkenaule |
| C. J. Kennedy | main St. Killenaule |
| E O Sullewan | killenaule |
| Con Yokes | Galbertston Holy Cross Thurles |
| Mrs Gleesan | Galbertston Holy Cross Thurles |

NOTE—The execution has been fixed for the 23rd April, 1941, and, accordingly, it is essential that all Reprieve Forms should reach Henry Gleeson's Solicitor, Mr. JOHN J. TIMONEY, LL.B., St. Michael's Street, Tipperary, as soon as possible.

Pages from the petition to save Harry Gleeson from the gallows. The last two signatures on the first page are those of Harry Gleeson's

# PETITION FOR REPRIEVE OF HENRY GLEESON

WE, the undersigned, hereby humbly request the Government, pursuant to the provisions of the Constitution of Ireland, to advise the President to commute the sentence of death passed upon Henry Gleeson in the Central Criminal Court on the 27th day of March, 1941.

| NAME | ADDRESS |
|---|---|
| Mrs W Dwyer | Dogstown Cashel. |
| Bridget Cagney | Killenastana |
| Winifred O Dwyer | Dogstown. Cashel. |
| John Caesar. | Marlhill Cahir. |
| Bridget Ceaser | Marlhill Cahir |
| Thomas Reid | Marlhill Cahir |
| Edmond Shehan | Marlhill Cahir |
| O. O'Shea | Co. 24 South Terrace, Cork |
| John Priorley | Courtmille Tipperary |
| | |
| | |
| | |

NOTE—The execution has been fixed for the 23rd April, 1941, and, accordingly, it is essential that all Reprieve Forms should reach Henry Gleeson's Solicitor, Mr. JOHN J. TIMONEY, LL.B., St. Michael's Street, Tipperary, as soon as possible.

mother Catherine and his cousin Con Vokes; John and Bridget Caesar's signatures are on the second. COURTESY NATIONAL ARCHIVES

On 16 April, Timoney submitted some signed petitions to the Department of Justice, saying that lack of time prevented the collection of more signatures. A day earlier, he had submitted a 25-page summary written in layman's English, setting out the problems with the conviction of Harry Gleeson, more than likely a version of the document submitted to the Attorney General, Kevin Haugh.

Some 7,000 people signed the petition, including Fine Gael's Colonel Jerry Ryan TD; Seán Ó Glasain (Gleeson), chairman of Thurles Urban District Council; Tipperary solicitors James F. D'Arcy and James Leamy; Father Michael Twomey OSA, Fethard; Father Ailbe Sadlier, Abbot of Roscrea Abbey;[6] and John J. Shanahan, secretary of the Clonmel Co-operative Society. John and Bridget Caesar signed it too, along with Tommy Reid and many of their neighbours. Other signatories included Con Kearney, who had been jailed for a sexual assault on Moll's daughter Mary McCarthy and who had fathered Moll's son Cornelius or Connie. Frank Loughman TD signed it – as a close associate of Hennessy and Nagle he had better reason than most to know that Gleeson was innocent. He knew, from a long way back, that his former IRA associates Nagle and Hennessy had 'guilty knowledge' of the arson attack on the McCarthy cottage, and must have known that Gleeson was innocent. Michael J. Davern, who later became Fianna Fáil TD for South Tipperary, wrote a letter pleading for clemency 'for this poor fellow'. Davern's son Noel, who succeeded him as a TD, tried to reopen the case in the 1990s. Noel Davern died while this book was being researched. He told me that 'Mick [his father] and Bridgie [Bridget] Caesar were forever discussing the case and trying to get something done for Harry.'[7] A surviving signatory pointed out to me that the petition sought only the lifting of the death penalty, and did not address the question of innocence or guilt. She had signed it hoping to save Gleeson's life, but she was not fully convinced of his innocence. Copies of the petition would continue to arrive in the Department of Justice after Harry Gleeson was hanged.

Meanwhile, Taoiseach Éamon de Valera formally met people pleading for a reprieve for Gleeson, following Mike Ryan's intervention. The Taoiseach was accompanied by a chief superintendent called Sheridan and Superintendent O'Mahony. The Taoiseach said he had asked the chief superintendent to examine the file. He had done so, and solemnly assured the Taoiseach that Gleeson had been convicted correctly. In those circumstances, de Valera said, his hands were tied; he could do nothing.

Before the hanging could take place, the government had to consider the jury's plea for clemency. On 8 April 1941, Department of Justice official Peter Berry wrote to the secretary of the government saying that the hanging was set for 23 April, and asking that the matter be scheduled for discussion at the next cabinet meeting.[8] Berry, who was private secretary to Minister for Justice Gerry Boland, enclosed for circulation to ministers O'Mahony's infamous report of 3 March. Notes on the margins of the file indicate the displeasure of the Department of the Taoiseach at this breach of procedure. Assistant secretary of the Taoiseach's department Pádraig Ó Cinnéide quickly instructed Berry to produce a proper memorandum for government, and not to rely on the O'Mahony document, which was recalled and destroyed, according to the file.[9] Peter Berry belatedly set about producing a civil service memorandum reciting the facts of the case for ministers to consider at their meeting on 16 April.

As late as 13 April 1941, Easter Sunday, Sergeant Reynolds and Garda Scully went with Patrick McCarthy once more to the Caesar farm, and Patrick was asked to point out where he had searched for his mother on the night she had disappeared. This was after the appeal had been lost, and just ten days before Harry was hanged.

Ministers met on Wednesday, 16 April, and considered Peter Berry's replacement[10] for the O'Mahony document. The replacement memorandum drafted by Peter Berry was better in some ways than the O'Mahony version, but nonetheless it contained tendentious and damaging assertions not proven in court:

> Michael McCarthy asked if there were any potatoes for dinner [on Wednesday 20 November]. She [Moll] replied that there were not, but that she was getting a 'butt' [sack] of potatoes that night from Harry Gleeson at the dug-out – that she had given him a sack for them the previous day, and that he was to get them for her while his aunt and uncle were away that day.

Ministers also heard that the trial judge, Martin Maguire, had told Gerald Boland confidentially that the conviction was sound. A letter was produced from

Maguire to the Department of Justice that rubbished any question of clemency.

> I can recall nothing in this case which would lead me to doubt that the verdict of the jury was correct and just. With regard to the recommendation of the jury I am not aware of anything in the case on which this recommendation can be fairly and justly grounded. The murder was one of exceptional brutality. The motive which appears to have actuated the crime was sordid and of a type full of danger to the public peace. The victim was a quiet inoffensive woman struggling hard to rear her six illegitimate children.
>
> I am unable to recall any extenuating circumstance, or redeeming feature, in the conduct of the prisoner in this very grave case.[11]

So ministers decided that the law should take its course. A report in *The Irish Times* of Saturday, 19 April 1941, said that the government had turned down the petition for Harry Gleeson's reprieve and he would be hanged on the following Wednesday.

The atmosphere in Mountjoy Jail on the days coming up to Harry's hanging was described by a prisoner, Walter Mahon-Smith, a former bank official whose gambling had been his undoing:

> While I was a prisoner in Mountjoy, a man was hanged. When the man left the dock under sentence of death, he was taken downstairs and searched to the skin. From that moment until he was dead, he was under constant supervision of warders.

The warders work in pairs, in eight-hour shifts, and not for one moment is a condemned murderer out of their sight. They accompany him on exercise and sit on chairs with him in the condemned cell playing cards or other games. At night, the light is lowered and the warders sit at the table keeping the convict in bed under constant surveillance. They make tea for him during the night if he feels like it. The doomed man is given any food he desires, provided the prison doctor sanctions it. He can have an occasional bottle of stout and plenty of cigarettes. He is visited daily by Sisters of Charity, and near the end he can have morning Mass and Communion.

This man [Gleeson] who was hanged during my time in Mountjoy told the hangman and warders present at his execution that he would pray for them that night in paradise. He had absolute faith. One of the warders who guarded him on his last night told me that this murderer said he felt exactly the same as he had felt on the morning he had made his first holy communion thirty years before. 'A nice holy feeling, not exactly understanding what lay ahead.'[12]

The hangman was Albert Pierrepoint, brought over from England to carry out the executions. It was said of him that he approached his job in as humane a way as was possible. Using the weight of the prisoner, he was able to calculate what drop was required to accomplish a clean break of the neck, thus shortening the individual's agony. Attempts to train an Irish hangman had not been successful.

Mahon-Smith's account continued:

> The tenseness grew, the air seemed charged with electricity, the strain reached breaking point. I never experienced such a sensation; 500 prisoners, and everyone connected with the prison, from the highest officer to the youngest child of a warder, all in a state of suspended apprehension – waiting – waiting – waiting – waiting: while in the condemned cell, the central figure of the nerve storm was praying aloud: 'Father, forgive them, for they know not what they do.'
>
> At last, the dread day dawned. From an early hour, we, first offenders, were on our knees reciting rosaries for the doomed man. As eight o'clock approached, his time on earth became shorter; an hour, ten minutes, a minute. At last as the bell of a neighbouring church tolled the fatal hour we knew a life was passing out.

One who heard the bell of St Peter's Church in Phibsboro at eight o'clock on Wednesday, 23 April 1941, was Gráinne Kavanagh, who was getting ready to leave for school. Her father was the prison governor, and she and her older sister Nola, along with their parents Betty and Seán Kavanagh, lived in the 'big house' in the prison grounds.

'Being children, we weren't supposed to know about the hangings but we always did; we found out somehow,' she told me. 'Athair [Father] hated them … he always went quiet in the weeks before a hanging. He used to spend a lot of time with the man in the death cell. And when he came back, we knew that's where he had been because he used to whistle, whistle quietly to himself.'[13]

The atmosphere in The Reynard public house in New Inn was very sombre on the night after Harry was hanged. Three off-duty gardaí – Frank Gralton, Vincent Scully and another – were present, drinking at the bar when a local man Jim Carew came in. Carew, a friend of Harry Gleeson, accused the policemen of being responsible for hanging an innocent man. Words were traded, then blows. Between them, the three gardaí were unable to overcome Carew, and they left.

# 6. Aftermath

In the days following the hanging, two letters describing Gleeson's last hours made their way from Dublin to County Tipperary. Anastasia Cooney received a letter from a priest at Holy Cross College, Clonliffe, who had been with the condemned man on the morning of his execution. 'You will be glad, though not surprised, that our friend Henry Gleeson made a most edifying end today. He slept peacefully during the night, and had to be awakened this morning. I gave him the Last Blessing and we began to recite his favourite ejaculations [short prayers]. He answered these bravely right up to the end.' The letter was signed by a Father John Kelly, who also said that Gleeson had made his last confession and received communion on the morning of his death. 'He has promised not to forget us who are here below and to help us when our time comes.'

Another letter, written on the same day, was addressed to John Timoney in Tipperary town from Seán MacBride in Dublin. MacBride explained to Gleeson's solicitor that he had got a message from the prison on the day before the hanging, saying that Harry wanted to speak to him. Like the prison chaplain, MacBride found Gleeson composed and untroubled by his fate. He told MacBride that he would never be so well prepared for death as he was then.

As MacBride took his leave of his client, Gleeson said:

> The last thing I want to say is that I will pray
> tomorrow that whoever did it will be discovered,
> and that the whole thing will be like an open
> book. I rely on you then to clear my name. I have
> no confession to make, only that I didn't do it.
> That is all. I will pray for you and be with you if
> I can, whenever you and Mr Nolan-Whelan and
> Mr Timoney are fighting and battling for justice.

After MacBride left the cell, he went to his car where he made a verbatim note of those remarks, to share them with Timoney.

Back at Marlhill, Harry Gleeson's younger brother Paddy had stepped in to run the farm for John Caesar, in time inheriting it, as Harry might have done.

A little later, Tommy Reid had a chance encounter with Garda Frank Gralton on a bus travelling to New Inn. Gralton told him that Gleeson had admitted his guilt to his cellmates in Limerick jail, and Gralton also managed to get in a jibe about Mrs Caesar being fond of a drink. Tommy Reid changed seats on the bus to get away from Gralton.

On 9 May 1941, District Justice Troy made an order at Cashel District Court committing the four younger McCarthy children to industrial schools. To his credit, he had refused applications to remove the children while Moll McCarthy was alive, but now he had little choice. He did not have to add a ringing endorsement of the behaviour of the police. *The Irish Times* reported that Troy spoke highly of the way in which the case had been conducted by the gardaí. 'I wish the clerk [of the court] to convey to the authorities my deep appreciation of the work of the chief superintendent [Edward Reynolds] and Superintendent O'Mahony.'

In June 1941, O'Mahony revoked John Caesar's firearms licence and attempted to confiscate his shotgun, but he later relented and allowed him to sell the weapon.

Tommy Reid's claim for damages arising out of the assault by Chief Superintendent Edward Reynolds and Detective Sergeant James Reynolds in New Inn garda station began in Dublin on 31 October 1941. Bridget Caesar gave evidence that when she said to Superintendent O'Mahony that it was a shame to have beaten Reid, he replied, 'You often heard tell of a good beating to knock a thing out of a fellow.' The gardaí gave what can only be described as perjured evidence, and Reid lost his case. A little later, Reid appears to have had a nervous breakdown, and he went to live with his sister in Dublin.

Nobody seemed to notice the next time the Gleeson trial surfaced in print, since those responsible took great care to cover their tracks. In 1945, author Maurice Walsh published a novel *The Man in Brown* – the plot of which draws heavily on the trial of Harry Gleeson.[1] Walsh is now best known for his short story 'The Quiet Man' and the film version starring John Wayne and Maureen O'Hara, released in 1952, which has been such a boon to the Irish tourist industry. *The Man in Brown* is dedicated to Walsh's fellow writer and drinking buddy David Sears. In the dedication Walsh says to Sears 'you told me the original of the story'. And that story was largely Moll McCarthy and Harry Gleeson's story, because Sears' day job was that of court reporter for the *Irish Independent*. Walsh and Sears both appear in *Dublin Culture* in Alan Reeves' famous cartoon of the capital's literary set, gathered in the Palace Bar in Fleet Street. Sears' play *The Dead Ride East* had been staged in the Gate Theatre in Dublin in 1931, with Orson Welles in the cast.

Letters from Sears to Walsh in the University of Limerick archives show how the two stories were first meshed, and then the links were concealed. Maurice Walsh had begun writing a novel about a man tried three times for the same murder. Walsh commissioned Sears to write a draft for his novel of the court scenes, based on the Gleeson trial. He wanted them to be authentic, but at the same time the origins of the story had to be concealed. 'I wrote on the principle that everyone connected with the Gleeson case would study our story to see if there was any possibility that he could take an action against us for libel,' Sears wrote to Walsh in a letter.

Reading the drafts Sears sent to Walsh is like reading the court transcript all over again. Dr Guiney, the local doctor, is Dr O'Connor; Dr Hartigan is Dr McGrath, the state pathologist.[2] Shots are heard at 5.40 p.m. and Sears reminds Walsh that that 'gives us a margin of about 15 hours in which we can stage our real murder any time we like'. This of course is the same unresolved question at the heart of Harry Gleeson's trial. As Sears drafted it, there is a dog lying on the body when it is found, and the body temperature Dr Guiney measures is 96 degrees

Fahrenheit, the same as that recorded by Dr O'Connor when he examined Moll McCarthy's body in the field.

In Sears' account, the accused arrived at the barracks to report finding the body at 9.20 a.m., having discovered it at 8.45 a.m. (Here we must adjust for the one hour difference between new and old time.) Even the dates – 20th and 21st – are the same.

Sears was providing details for Walsh to incorporate into his story, three years after Harry Gleeson had been hanged, but the legal risks of importing details of a real trial continued to bother the friends. Between drafting and publication, many of Sears' suggestions based on the similarities to the Gleeson case were removed, although the basic plot elements of farm manager, two shots heard, murder and inheritance remain. In the last letter of this passage of his correspondence with Walsh, Sears lists forty-three names from the 1941 trial which must *not* be given to fictional characters, starting with Gleeson, Nolan-Whelan, and garbling the name of witness Martin Vokes. He also drafted a disclaimer to be signed by Maurice Walsh: 'This is not an attempt to retell H—G—'s story ... the medical facts are on record, and the whole of my story is imaginary.'

On the surface, *The Man in Brown*, published in the United States as *Nine Strings to Your Bow*, bears little to link it with Harry Gleeson and Moll McCarthy's story, and, as far as I could trace, reviewers and readers missed the connection.

The real significance of Sears being in court throughout the Gleeson trial lies in his recognition that the accused had told some lies in evidence and the jury knew this. In a fictional passage drafted by

Sears, a private detective asks the accused why he should take on the case, given that the man had lied in court. 'The defendant replies that he lied about nothing affecting his own guilt.' That was the verdict on Harry Gleeson on the press bench – but not in the jury room – on 27 February 1941.

Some years after Harry Gleeson's hanging, a local man encountered Sergeant Anthony Daly in unusual circumstances. The man was Bill O'Connor and in his book he describes an occasion between 1941 and 1947 (when Daly retired and left New Inn) on which Bill had gone to a dance in New Inn with his sister May and her friend Katie Tobin. For a while Bill devoted his attention to a 'gorgeous blonde' but too soon the dance was over. Bill O'Connor had difficulty starting the car he had arrived in, a Ford 14.9, a version of the Model A, which had been converted to run on paraffin because of wartime petrol rationing.

When he finally got it started, Daly appeared from nowhere and told Bill to switch off the engine and go with him to Barron's pub in New Inn for a drink. Bill protested: it was too late, he had no money, and he had to drive his sister and Katie Tobin home. Daly insisted and, since Bill had neither tax nor insurance on the car, he went with him, insisting that he had no money, nor had the two women. The men sat at one end of the taproom, the women at the other end.[3] Daly bought a succession of large whiskies for himself and small ones for Bill O'Connor.

Eventually, Daly got to the point. Seven cattle had been stolen in the area and the station sergeant was under pressure to solve the crime. Daly thought Bill O'Connor had information about this.

As the drinking continued, Daly began to boast about the number of spies and informers he had tabs on in New Inn, and in other places where he had been posted. Then, according to Bill O'Connor, Anthony Daly said, 'Wasn't it easy for us [the gardaí] to be waiting for Harry Gleeson, the morning he came to the barracks to report a murder. I had been informed between 11.30 p.m. and midnight that Moll McCarthy had been shot in a field of Caesar's and that it was Harry Gleeson who shot her.' He mentioned the man who carried the message, but Bill O'Connor did not name him.

Bill O'Connor eventually privately published his own account of these events calling it *The Farcical Trial of Harry Gleeson.* In his own words, Bill O'Connor, known as 'The Billo', had left school a 'total dunce'. He worked at building and other trades, and while recuperating from a serious injury on a building site in England, resolved that, if he recovered, he would do his best to clear his friend and neighbour Harry Gleeson's name. It is worth mentioning that Bill O'Connor appears to endorse the belief that those who carried out the murder were not from New Inn.

Daly's bravado during this boozing session may be just that, owing more to drink than fact, but its lasting effect was to encourage Bill O'Connor to continue his investigations and eventually to attract Marcus Bourke and other writers to ask questions about Gleeson's hanging.

John Caesar died ten years after Harry, but Bridget lived on for a further twenty years in the farmhouse at Marlhill. She continued to campaign to clear Harry's name until her death on 11 March 1972.

Later that year, in the December 1972 edition of *The Word*, a Catholic monthly magazine, Seán MacBride was asked if he ever lost a legal case where an innocent man was hanged. He replied, 'A man was tried for the murder of a woman in County Tipperary. He was convicted on what I regarded as completely insufficient evidence.' MacBride then described the last interview in the condemned cell. 'I was shattered. I was quite certain that the man was innocent.'

MacBride was talking to Brother Paul Hurley SVD, the remarkable founder and editor of *The Word* magazine. Paul Hurley pioneered what was then a new form of magazine journalism, matching words and colour pictures to tell vivid stories, and *The Word* won the admiration of secular and religious journalists alike, and readers worldwide. MacBride also mentioned the Gleeson case in an article by journalist Vincent Browne in 1974. 'He didn't commit the crime ... because he was elsewhere at the time.'[4] The significance of that remark – where was Harry Gleeson and how did MacBride know – escaped the scrutiny it merited at that time.

In fact, MacBride had adverted to the Gleeson hanging earlier, as the Department of Justice had noted. In January 1963, Minister for Justice Charles Haughey unexpectedly announced that the government was considering abolishing capital punishment. Welcoming this, MacBride observed in a TV appearance that he had acted in a case where a man was wrongly hanged, but without mentioning the name. By now secretary of the Department of Justice, the ever-vigilant Peter Berry spotted this and wrote in the following terms to his minister on 30 January, enclosing the relevant file:

This is probably the case about which Seán MacBride said recently (on TV and in the press) that as counsel he had a very strong feeling that the accused had not committed the murder. It is the only murder case which he defended since 1940, apart from the political cases in which there could be no doubt whatsoever about the guilt of the accused.

On the other hand (and this could not be said publicly) the State had the best of reasons for knowing that Gleeson committed the murder.

As you will see from the papers, MacBride fought very hard for a reprieve and government refused.

The underlining is in Berry's handwriting, and his meaning remains unexplained. Was this a reference to the alleged confession in Limerick Jail, never mentioned in court, or is Berry referring to something else?

With the passage of time, a more measured examination of events in Ireland's recent past was becoming possible. On 15 August 1987, in St Patrick's College, Thurles, a group of sixteen people from various disciplines gathered. The purpose was to discuss publishing a historical journal for the whole county. The County Tipperary Historical Society was inaugurated on that day. Local historian Eddie Dalton became chairman, and academic Willie Nolan was elected vice-chairman. Other officers included journalist and barrister Marcus Bourke, and historians Liam Ó Duibhir and Denis Marnane. Though the remit of the new society embraced a wide range of cultural, historical and social matters, the three first named, Dalton, Nolan and Bourke, would be responsible for publishing the first forensic examination of the Harry Gleeson trial, *Murder at Marlhill*, in 1993: Marcus Bourke, biographer of John O'Leary and historian of the Gaelic Athletic Association, as author; Eddie Dalton as researcher; and Willie Nolan as publisher, through his imprint Geography Publications.

Someone drew Marcus Bourke's attention to *The Farcical Trial of Harry Gleeson*, about fifty copies of which were in circulation in south Tipperary in 1990. Bill O'Connor, whose encounter with Anthony Daly is described above, was a cousin of the doctor who first examined Moll McCarthy's body in the field. Essentially, O'Connor had compiled an annotated version of the newspaper reports of the trial that culminated in the death sentence, drawing attention to the parts that defy belief. The appearance of his book is uninviting: 120 foolscap pages of crudely duplicated and unevenly spaced type. The grammar is wobbly but, though the annotations are uneven, many are to the point. In summary, the book consists of a series of hammer blows to the credibility of the conviction.

At last, the pieces of the jigsaw that would eventually lead to Harry Gleeson's innocence being accepted were falling into place. Bill O'Connor had highlighted the main flaws in the conviction and some members of the group behind the newly formed County Tipperary Historical Society, but acting on their own behalf, had the skills to investigate further and put together a cogent case for Gleeson's innocence.

Bourke – with the help of Eddie Dalton's research – began to make progress. The Knockgraffon school register was obtained and it yielded important information about the whereabouts of Michael and Nellie McCarthy on the day their mother went missing. Eddie Dalton traced the register of ammunition sales in Feehan's shop in Cashel and it showed clear signs of having been tampered with. Then, in 1992, Marcus Bourke and others visited Tommy Reid.

Reid, living in retirement in County Waterford, was still angry about his treatment at the hands of gardaí. As they sat in his living room, Reid told his visitors that Gleeson had lied when he said he did not recognise Moll McCarthy's body lying in the field when he had first seen it. When Gleeson told Mrs Caesar about finding the body in the field, she had told him to report it to the gardaí, but not to say that he had recognised the victim. And Tommy Reid had another surprise in store. On the afternoon of Wednesday, 20 November 1940, not long before the last sighting of Moll McCarthy, Reid had been milking cows in a field adjoining the lane, or boreen, linking Caesar's farmhouse with the main road. He stopped to rest with the heavy pails for a moment and noticed a 'man in jodphurs' watching him from the 'mouth of the lane'. (In New Inn the 'man in jodphurs' was taken to mean Caesar's neighbour Patrick or Paddy Byrne, who had served in the Irish army; the jodphurs had once been part of his uniform.)

The man did not speak but withdrew behind the hedge, as Reid picked up his pails again and went towards the farmyard. A little later, Reid went to wash his hands at a tank in the yard, where Gleeson, who had come from the ploughing, was doing the same. The time was between 6.30 and 7 p.m., probably closer to 7 p.m., he said. As he did, he heard two shots ring out in the dark. 'By God, whoever fired those shots must have cat's eyes,' Reid said to Gleeson, who did not reply. After dusk, it is almost impossible to fire a shotgun with any degree of accuracy. Reid later wondered if Harry had heard those shots, because of his deafness.

When Reid finished talking, one of those present asked him if he had told anyone about this incident. Reid replied that he had told Mrs Caesar.

When Gleeson got back from the barracks and all the gardaí had left, except one who was standing guard over the body in the stubble field, Bridget Caesar called Gleeson and Tommy Reid into the house and questioned them closely about what they knew. When she learned about the shots Reid had heard, she issued her orders, as she always did in that house. They were both in the clear and they were to say nothing to the gardaí, and were to stay away from the gardaí, too, if they could manage it. It was bad advice, but Bridget Caesar was trying to defend her own little family unit as her world imploded around her. She could not know that Gleeson would become ensnared in a tangled web not entirely of his or her making. Now the Caesars could not be called to give evidence of Harry Gleeson's good character for fear of making a liar of him.

After *Murder at Marlhill* was published in 1993, it was no longer possible to argue that Gleeson had been fairly convicted on the evidence. Manifestly he had not, but three interlocking questions remained:

had Gleeson really murdered Moll McCarthy? Did the gardaí have to fabricate evidence to get a conviction? And if Gleeson really was innocent, who had killed Moll McCarthy?

In 2009, the last full year of his life, Marcus Bourke said that he had wished to name those responsible for murdering Moll McCarthy when writing *Murder at Marlhill*, but he was persuaded not to do so, in deference to local sensitivities.[5] However, Bourke said he was convinced that Jack Nagle and Thomas Hennessy were involved in Moll's murder, and he included their names in the first chapter of his book, minus a direct accusation. He intended this as a pointer to anyone who wanted to know more.

Following publication of the book, people who could add to the story contacted Marcus Bourke. Some wished to congratulate him, others to add information. And at least one was curious about how he had reached his conclusions. Among Bourke's papers are notes for a new chapter for a revised edition of *Murder at Marlhill*, incorporating the new material.[6]

Perhaps the most significant endorsement of his book came from a retired assistant garda commissioner, Dan Devitt. He wrote to express his revulsion at the behaviour of the senior officers involved – whom he must have known – and his unquestioning acceptance of the facts as set forth by Marcus Bourke is very significant. Police forces worldwide are known for their unwillingness to criticise their own.

Dan Devitt's letter, dated 6 January 1994, congratulated Bourke on vindicating Harry Gleeson's good name, and said 'the investigation of the case throws a dark shadow over the reputation of the [garda] force'. Devitt, who had Tipperary connections but had spent his forty-two years as a policeman in Dublin and County Louth, singled out Chief Superintendent Edward Reynolds and Superintendent Patrick O'Mahony for particular censure. He said that other members of the force were obliged only to carry out *lawful* orders from superiors (his emphasis). Devitt said that he had served for many years as a station sergeant and he would never have allowed a case as weak as that to go to trial. The standard procedure was that the prosecuting garda put the evidence to the station sergeant for a decision on whether or not to proceed. The case against Gleeson was far too flimsy to be sent forward, Devitt said. He was distressed by the outcome and what it said about the forces of law and order in which he had served for most of his working life.

It was a frank statement from a former senior garda. Devitt was no liberal. He had a reputation as a 'hardliner' and he supported the death penalty for the murder of a garda. He was on record as criticising liberal bail rules and concurrent jail sentences, which, he said, encouraged criminals to reoffend.

Probably the single most important new item of information in relation to the case came from a nurse, Anne Martin, who before her marriage had worked in a hospital in the Dublin suburb of Donnybrook. There, one of her charges was Moll McCarthy's eldest daughter, Mary, who, aged nineteen, had given evidence at Gleeson's trial. Thereafter Mary had spent her life in a Magdalene laundry working for nuns who had transferred her to hospital when she became unfit to continue laundry work.[7] Normally, a taciturn, even sullen, patient, Mary McCarthy became friendly with the woman who nursed her in her last illness. Late one night, while being tended by Nurse Martin, Mary confided that she had seen her mother killed on the kitchen floor, and that an innocent man had been hanged for the murder.

Below is the statement of Anne Martin:

In February 1988, I took up duty as a nurse in the Royal Hospital for Incurables in Donnybrook, Dublin 4. One of the patients there was Mary McCarthy of New Inn, County Tipperary, then 68 years of age and crippled by arthritis. I am from Fethard, County Tipperary, and because, I think, we were both from the same county, Mary and I became friendly. I learned that she had spent all her life from her teens onwards in convents, first in Cashel and later in Dublin. She was transferred to Donnybrook when she got into poor health and became immobile.

In the summer of 1988, I was on night duty with another nurse now living in Saudi Arabia. Mary McCarthy was in poor form, was crying and was generally upset. Suddenly one night she said to me: 'I saw my own mother shot on the kitchen floor.' Then she said something to the effect that 'an innocent man died'. Because I got such a shock at what she [had] said I cannot recall the exact words of her second sentence but I have never forgotten her first sentence. I think she told me about her mother because of our friendship, and she regretted not having told it to anyone before.

I told my colleague on night duty what Mary McCarthy had told me. I have recently contacted this colleague in Saudi Arabia and she has confirmed my account of the incident. At the next meeting in the hospital with my superiors, I reported the incident and asked if anybody knew anything about Mary's background, as I was new on the staff. I was told that she had lived her life in a convent and had no family. However I recall either one or two brothers of Mary visiting her from England, although it was clear to me that she did not want any contact with the family. I also remember a nun visiting her from a convent in Dublin where Mary had worked; her name was Sister Luke. I never later discussed her family with Mary.

Some time in late 1989 or early 1990 Mary McCarthy died at the age of 69. I was then off duty, but when I returned she was in the hospital morgue. I contacted Sister Luke and asked for Mary to be buried in the convent cemetery, but she said it was full, so she was buried in Glasnevin. I was at the funeral. None of Mary's family attended.

When I visited my home in County Tipperary after the incident, I told my mother, and she said that she had a vague memory of the case as a child. New Inn is only about 10 miles from my home in Moyglass near Fethard. She told me that a man had been executed for the murder of Mary's mother and there had been dissatisfaction locally, because people doubted if the gardaí had got the right man.

# Aftermath

When the book *Murder at Marlhill* came out last Christmas my mother told me about it on a visit home. She said that whoever wrote it did not know where Mary McCarthy (senior) had been murdered, as it did not mention that story that Mary McCarthy (junior) had told me. My mother urged me to contact those involved in the book so I contacted Mr Eddie Dalton of Golden, who is mentioned in the introduction. I then visited him at his home and told him of the incident in the hospital. He told me that there had been no news of Mary McCarthy for years and that nobody in New Inn knew she was dead.

I understand from the book or from Eddie Dalton or Marcus Bourke that Mary McCarthy was said to have been mentally retarded. I do not accept this. While I knew her she was not in any way retarded. She remained mentally alert to the end and was quite an intelligent woman, with clear and often bitter views on her life and her family.

Signed Anne Martin, May 1994

Around the same time, broadcaster and senator Paschal Mooney had befriended Mary McCarthy. Mary was a country music fan and often wrote to Paschal Mooney with requests to play her favourite songs on his radio programme. Mooney had gone to visit her in hospital along with his broadcasting colleague Maggie Stapleton, and had managed to elicit from her that she was from 'near Cashel'. She did not discuss the murder with her visitors. However, Senator Mooney confirmed to me that Mary

McCarthy was *compos mentis* at the time he spoke to her.

If Mary McCarthy's statement to Nurse Martin was correct, its importance cannot be exaggerated. If her mother was killed in a kitchen, and if the police had known this, the entire prosecution case was built on a false foundation. This could have happened in any farmhouse nearby, though we can only guess at possible reasons for Mary and her mother being there. The prosecution case that Harry had an appointment with her on the Wednesday evening in the stubble field – and it had no direct evidence of this – and killed her there can be ruled out.

What now is one to make of witness Thomas Hennessy's story of the two shots he heard as he pushed his bicycle across the fields; and what of the shots from a double-barrelled shotgun heard by the tailor Joseph Moloney on the Thursday morning? More importantly, if the killing was done in front of the nineteen-year-old daughter, where were Moll's two older sons (Patrick aged fifteen and Michael aged twelve) at the time?

Nobody who saw and heard Anne Martin's testimony given in a TV documentary[8] in 1995 could have any doubt about her sincerity, and its implications for the prosecution case against Harry Gleeson. When I spoke to her by phone in the summer of 2013, she confirmed that nothing had happened in the intervening years to cause her to add or subtract from her statement.

In a draft chapter for an updated edition of *Murder at Marlhill*, which was never published, Marcus Bourke wrote of having received information stating that Sergeant Anthony Daly had much to answer for in the wrongful conviction of Harry Gleeson. 'Curiously, none of the information regarding Sergeant Daly as having masterminded the murder suggests that he actually shot Moll McCarthy,' Bourke wrote. 'However, from three different sources, it is possible now to suggest who in fact did the actual killing,' he continued. 'In a thinly-disguised message I received from a retired guard, it was suggested to me that one of the local group identified both for me, and for Father James Meehan, parish priest of New Inn when he carried out his inquiries,[9] "borrowed" the shotgun merely by walking into Caesar's yard and making away with it when the place was deserted.'

Marcus Bourke identified Patrick J. (Pak) O'Gorman as the man who fired the fatal shot. He made this charge in public twice: once on a TG4 dramatised documentary *Ceart agus Cóir*, broadcast on 2 February 2006,[10] and in a signed note placed in the National Archives file on the trial of Henry Gleeson, where I found it on 2 February 2012.

The memoriam card which accompanies the note bears a prayer of St Monica: *All I ask of you is that wherever you may be, you will remember me at Holy Communion, and at the foot of the Altar.* The date 18 April 1997 indicates that the note was placed in the National Archives file after Marcus Bourke had given up hope that a pardon for Harry Gleeson would be granted. This note has now been removed from the National Archives file, because, according to an archivist, it does not belong with the documentation of the trial.

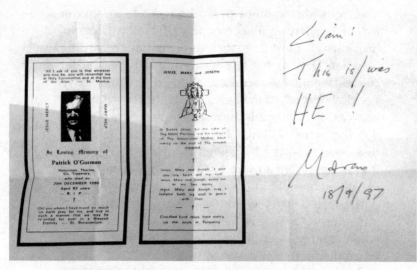

The note accusing Patrick J. O'Gorman, also known as Pak O'Gorman, of firing the shot which killed Moll, signed by Marcus Bourke and found in the National Archives file on the trial of Harry Gleeson in 2012. The Liam to whom it was addressed is not known. COURTESY KIERAN FAGAN

Pak O'Gorman was a good mechanic – in the broad sense of the word. He was good with his hands and could fix almost anything mechanical. In 2012 I spoke to a man who recalled Pak O'Gorman converting a damaged double-barrelled shotgun to single barrel use, a considerable feat of amateur engineering. He owned a flat-back lorry and neighbours hired him to move livestock and goods. This lorry was hired by gardaí to move Moll McCarthy's body from the field where it lay to New Inn garda station for the state pathologist's examination, according to members of the Gleeson family. Pak was eleven at the time of the 1911 census. He was a brother of William, who lived on the family farm at Ardnassa, bordering John Caesar's farm.

When Pak O'Gorman grew up, he left New Inn and later ran a business near Holycross. He married twice, the second time in Holycross in the 1960s. Some New Inn sources thought that Pak O'Gorman had met Moll when she briefly lived and worked in Dublin. Marcus Bourke believed that while Pak O'Gorman was the man who fired the shot that killed Moll McCarthy, he was one of a group of men and not the ringleader. Note that Bourke did not accuse Pak O'Gorman of firing the subsequent shot that took away her face.

The notes for the updated but unpublished version of *Murder of Marlhill* contain the following passage regarding Pak O'Gorman: 'Furthermore, soon after the book appeared I [Marcus Bourke] learned indirectly that the same local man, when seriously ill some years ago, made what amounted to a deathbed confession to the killing – but then recovered. More recently I heard that a relative of this local man had openly claimed the killer as his relative ... Furthermore, I was told that it was this man's relative who had informed Sergeant Daly of the murder, the night before Gleeson found the body.'

During the original investigation, another New Inn resident, Jack Nagle, known locally as 'The Boss' Nagle, gave confidential statements to the police incriminating Harry Gleeson. It is likely that O'Mahony's self-justifying post-trial statement of the case drew on Nagle's briefings. In latter years, Nagle gave a statement of his 'National Activities' between 1914 and 1921 to the Bureau of Military History.[11] He had served as vice-commandant, 6th battalion,

3rd Tipperary Brigade of the IRA, and vice-officer commanding the Flying Column, he said. Aged about fifteen in 1914, he had first joined the Volunteer force of John Redmond, but when the Volunteers split, he went with Sinn Féin, at the suggestion of his neighbour Thomas Hennessy of Knockgraffon.

Apart from drilling and training, there had been no serious engagement with the enemy until 1920 when Nagle and others, including his neighbour Paddy Byrne of Knockgraffon, were sent with arms to ambush a patrol of Royal Irish Constabulary (RIC) men between Cashel and Golden. The ambush was in place, but the police never arrived. Soon after this, the brigade headquarters was set up in Rosegreen, about three miles from Hennessy's land, and some of the officers were billeted at Hennessy's – including local IRA leaders Seán Treacy[12] and Seán Hogan. A quarry on Hennessy's land was used to store arms and other supplies for the rebels. Soon afterwards, Seán Treacy gave Nagle responsibility for blocking roads and impeding supplies to barracks in the area. Then an RIC sergeant named Lee met Nagle in Downey's public house in New Inn, and tipped him off that he was about to be arrested. Nagle and Seán Hogan went on the run. Now Nagle was vice-commandant of the Flying Column, deployed whenever local intelligence officers detected movements of men and material. The task was to move swiftly and to tie down and cause maximum disruption to the forces of law and order.

Nagle's statement went on to describe exchanging fire with the Auxiliaries on a sweep through County Kilkenny; the standing down of the flying columns in the aftermath of the truce in 1922; his appointment

as vice-commander of the 3rd Tipperary Brigade and
his resignation from the IRA and return to farming at
Garrandee, New Inn, on 22 April 1922. He was then
just twenty-five years old.

In his twenty-five-page statement, signed in 1956,
Nagle identified his neighbours Patrick Byrne and
Thomas Hennessy as regular members of the Number
2 Flying Column. In time, all returned to their farms,
young men who had been 'blooded' in the service of
their country as they saw it, and who were disinclined
to take any form of authority at face value except their
own. Each had arms dumps on his land at some stage.
One on the former Byrne farm came to light just thirty
years ago. It had been a safe house for IRA men on the
run, as had the O'Gorman home nearby at Ardnassa.
The parish priest before Father O'Malley, Father
Edward Murphy, was a key member of the IRA
organisation in Tipperary, and it now looks certain
that Hennessy, Murphy and Nagle were complicit in
the episode in which Moll McCarthy's thatched roof
was set on fire.

Others who made contact with Marcus Bourke
had different stories to tell. A retired garda spoke of
a fellow garda, Michael Connolly, who had to type
all the documentation for the Gleeson trial. From
what he had read, he became convinced of Gleeson's
innocence. Connolly died in the late 1970s in County
Clare, according to Bourke.

Another source – Bourke describes him as a
'professional man' – was friendly with gardaí in Cahir
and they told him that it was common knowledge
among members of the force that Moll McCarthy
had not been killed where Harry Gleeson had found

her. Cahir was the headquarters of Superintendent O'Mahony who investigated Moll's murder. A retired solicitor who attended the Gleeson murder trial and Tommy Reid's later unsuccessful assault case told Marcus Bourke that he recalled overhearing gardaí stationed in Cahir discussing the murder in terms that acknowledged Sergeant Daly's role in covering up the matter.

Normally a copy of a murder investigation file is kept at garda divisional headquarters, in this case Thurles. However, in 1992, when Marcus Bourke sought it, the officer in charge had a search made for it without success. A bizarre explanation then emerged from a member of the Gleeson family. When Thurles garda station was being rebuilt in the 1950s, a contractor employed a cousin of Harry Gleeson. When transferring records from the old station he saw a box containing the Gleeson file. He managed to read the file over several sessions as the construction continued.

'Although [the informant is] now dead,' Marcus Bourke wrote, 'I was able to verify this story because his cousin could quote the substance of a secret garda memorandum which only became available in the National Archives when transferred there by the Department of the Taoiseach in 1994.'

The secret memorandum is the document prepared by Superintendent Patrick O'Mahony dated 3 March 1941, dealt with in chapter five, containing very derogatory allegations about the wider Gleeson family. During the term of office of Máire Geoghegan-Quinn as Minister for Justice 1993–94, Cashel-based TD Noel Davern asked her to reopen the Gleeson case. The Department of Justice then recalled two files on the subject from the National Archives, which were unavailable to researchers until December 2013, when the National Archives gave me access to the Department of the Taoiseach file, and subsequently to most of the Department of Justice file.

Those who campaign for a pardon for Harry Gleeson take as a starting point his consistent protestation of innocence. 'I had neither hand, act nor part' in the murder. And the Holy Grail for all those who have taken an interest in the case has been the letter that Harry is said to have written to his friend Pat Furlong from his prison cell, protesting his innocence. This letter is lost but Tim Godfrey[13] a nephew of Dolly Furlong, Pat's wife, had seen it, and he could recall what it said:

> Mountjoy Jail, 22nd April
> Pat
> Just a note to thank you and Dolly for all your help and kindness throughout thirty plus years. I thank you for your help at the farming on many occasions. I would also like to thank you for our partnership at half-field in Rockwell Rovers!
> I go to meet my God tomorrow morning. I am full prepared to do so. I have made my peace with God and I die an innocent man. I wish you both every happiness.
> Your friend
> Harry[14]

Although Tim Godfrey and his family were living in Wanstead, London, south Tipperary was their home and his children, Patricia and Tom, recalled happy holidays spent there. A maternal aunt, Dolly, along with her husband Pat, had reared Tim Godfrey after his mother died. Tim recalled discussing the Gleeson case with his aunt and her husband, and also with his father, a pharmacist in Cahir, who said he had raised his concerns about a miscarriage of justice when talking to Superintendent O'Mahony in the years following the hanging of Harry Gleeson.

However, Tim Godfrey's interest was rekindled when he found Marcus Bourke's book in a bookshop in Dún Laoghaire (he had travelled to Dublin to watch an international rugby match, in which Wales narrowly beat Ireland in Lansdowne Road on 4 February 1994). He set to work to try to find out more and engaged Stuart Price, a London-based private detective. Price tracked down Michael McCarthy, then in his sixties and working in the building trade in London. McCarthy agreed to be questioned for the RTÉ television documentary *Mystery at Marlhill*, broadcast on 23 November 1995, but added little to the general knowledge of the case.

However, when Michael was confronted with Nurse Anne Martin's account of Mary McCarthy saying that she had seen her mother killed on the kitchen floor, he dismissed this on the grounds that she was 'living out' at the time, meaning his sister was staying in the house of the woman who employed her. This conflicts with Mary's own sworn account of her movements given in 1940 and 1941. It is very strange that Michael should frame his rejection of the 'shooting in a kitchen' in these terms – not that it had not happened, but that Mary was not there to witness it. At the very least, this confirms my view that Michael McCarthy's testimony about dates and times was not to be trusted – not in the 1990s, and not in 1940 and 1941.

But he did make one interesting statement when interviewed for the TV documentary. When asked about Superintendent O'Mahony's disputed account of the conversation involving himself, his brother Patrick and Harry Gleeson, Michael said he had no recollection of it. If that exchange was fabricated – or largely fabricated – by O'Mahony, the so-called 'evidence' that Gleeson was Peggy's father, and that Moll had threatened to take Harry to court to pay maintenance is gone. The principal witness to that conversation said he had no recollection of it ever taking place.

There was another startling assertion in Marcus Bourke's notes for his revised edition. I quote the full text:

> From the son of a policeman involved in the investigation, interviewed shortly after *Murder at Marlhill* was published, came an astonishing admission. He clearly recalled his late father telling of tests carried out by his colleagues with [Thomas] Hennessy, prior to calling him as a witness. These had to be aborted because Hennessy frankly admitted that he heard no shots fired during the tests. Given this embarrassing situation, one can only charitably assume that Sergeant Daly's plans to base the charge of murder against Gleeson on Hennessy [would require him to] unscramble them by the

time they had learned of the tailor Moloney's story [of hearing shots on the Thursday morning] which got short shrift from the Court of Criminal Appeal.

The biggest hole in the prosecution case was its inability to say when the murder had taken place. The outline of Bourke's unpublished new chapter concludes with the speculation that John Caesar's isolation from the New Inn community was not just because of his being from another part of County Tipperary. His political views were at odds with his neighbours. Caesar was a 'Blueshirt', while his neighbours were staunch republicans. There is less support for the idea that his nephew Harry held the same crypto-fascist views. Harry's younger brother, Patrick (Paddy), who took over the Caesar farm and eventually inherited it in 1972 on the death of Bridget Caesar, was a member of the 2nd Tipperary Brigade of the Old IRA, according to a member of the extended Gleeson-Caesar family.

Marcus Bourke's further research took place between 1994, after his book was published, and includes the time when the RTÉ television documentary was broadcast in November 1995, and appears to have petered out before 2000. His file includes a cryptic note saying that IRA member George Plant – who had shot Michael Devereux in the head – was a 'customer' of Moll McCarthy, but no explanation of why he thought that. After that Bourke appears to have devoted his energies to a revised version of his history of the GAA, and his contributions to the *Dictionary of Irish Biography*.

In 2007, three years before he died, Marcus Bourke received a letter from a woman in County Meath called Mary Conmey. She had just read *Murder at Marlhill*. Her interest was whetted by the fact that her mother came from Cahir, and her family had a connection with Harry Gleeson. She wrote: 'You dedicated the book to Harry Gleeson's sister, Mary.[15] Mary Gleeson first met her husband on the journey to America. They met up later and eventually married. His name was Dan Gleeson and he was my mother's uncle on her father's side.'

Confusingly, there are two unrelated Gleesons marrying each other here. The important point is that Mary Conmey is related through her mother to Dan Gleeson, and is therefore not a blood relative of Mary or Harry Gleeson, but is related by marriage. And there was the link of being from Cahir. But there is another fascinating connection here.

Mary Conmey went on to say that her mother was seventeen when Harry Gleeson was hanged: 'My mother remembers the sombre atmosphere in her home at the time coming up to his execution.' And she recalled her mother being hostile to the Garda Síochána thereafter. She would have good reason.

Mary Conmey takes up the story:

> On 12th October 1971, a young nineteen-year-old County Meath woman named Una Lynskey went missing on her way home from work in Dublin. She was a neighbour of ours and had travelled home on the bus with her cousin. She had got off the bus at her cousin's house on the Fairyhouse road. She never arrived home and

the events that followed led to the very tragic death of a young nineteen-year-old man Martin Kerrigan.

Martin Kerrigan was abducted and killed by Una Lynskey's brothers Seán and James Lynskey and her cousin John Gaughan, nine days after her body was found. They had been led to believe that he was involved in her murder and this was their revenge. They were convicted of manslaughter as there was no evidence that Martin Kerrigan was dead when they left him on a remote mountain. He had been castrated.

After a heavy-handed garda investigation, two local men – Martin Conmey and Dick Donnelly – were convicted of the manslaughter of Una Lynskey. The investigation proved to be flawed – *inter alia* it did not give proper weight to an account of a Ford Zodiac car seen in the area, and reports of a woman answering Una Lynskey's description struggling with a man in the back of the car. A Ford Zodiac was an unusual and exotic car in the lanes of County Meath then, so people remembered it.

Mary Conmey, who wrote to Marcus Bourke in 2007, had married Paraic Gaughan, a cousin of Una Lynskey's, in 1976. In 2007, her brother Martin Conmey was pursuing a case through the Court of Criminal Appeal to have his conviction for the manslaughter of Una Lynskey overturned. Dick Donnelly's conviction for manslaughter was overturned on appeal in 1973, but not Martin Conmey's, and he had served three years in jail for a crime he did not commit. Martin Conmey's conviction was eventually overturned in 2010, and in July 2014 that conviction was certified as a 'miscarriage of justice'. Nothing could be done for Martin Kerrigan, killed at the age of nineteen in revenge for a crime he did not commit.

There was another link to the Moll McCarthy case. In 1973, Mary Conmey's parents had sought a meeting with Seán MacBride, who was then chairman of Amnesty International's executive committee. They had turned to him for help when all their attempts for justice through the court system had failed. MacBride treated them with courtesy and compassion and gave whatever advice he could. In her letter to him, Mary Conmey asked Marcus Bourke if he could help her in locating any record of her parents' meeting with MacBride. He had none. Enclosed with this letter was a photograph of Harry Gleeson's sister Mary on her first visit to Ireland since emigrating to the United States in the 1920s. Taken in 1957 in County Tipperary, it shows her with a large white or cream American car she and her husband had shipped over. When researching this book a quarter of a century later, I spoke to people who remembered that large American car being driven around the county, even though the identity of the owner was forgotten.

'It is a sad reflection on the gardaí and our justice system that my mother should be touched twice in her lifetime by separate miscarriages of justice,' Mary Conmey observed.

So what do we now know about what happened on the night of Wednesday, 20 November 1940?

We know that Moll McCarthy went out to meet someone, probably in Lynch's disused farmhouse, less than half a mile from the Caesars' house. She had taken a diagonal route across the Caesars' fields, walking in a north-easterly direction towards the Mass path shortcut from Marlhill to New Inn. She crossed the ditch from which Harry Gleeson saw her body the next day.

We simply do not know when she was killed. Between midnight and about 5 a.m. or 6 a.m. on Thursday morning her body was taken to the stubble field where it was found. There, the shot that removed her face was fired. Moll was not wearing her coat when the first shot was fired, but had been neatly buttoned into it after she died.

So why was Harry Gleeson hanged for her murder? Because, as his lead barrister James Nolan-Whelan said, he was the 'most unfortunate man in the country'. Gleeson walked into it. Because when he found the body, he told a lie. He recognised Moll McCarthy lying in the field but when he went to the police station to report it, he said he did not know who she was. He told some other white lies to protect others. The jury spotted at least one lie, and suspected there were others.

Most importantly, Gleeson was an outsider – along with his uncle and aunt by marriage, John and Bridget Caesar. When Caesar needed a carpenter, he sent for a kinsman living at Galbertstown, instead of employing a local man. That pattern of behaviour reinforced the isolation of the Caesars in Marlhill. And the entire Gleeson-Caesar-Hogan clan were outsiders. Bridget Caesar (née Hogan) was from near Tipperary town, the Caesars and Gleesons from Galbertstown, near Holycross to the north. If the overused phrase 'tight-knit' ever applied to a community, it did to the residents of Marlhill and Knockgraffon and the other townlands around New Inn. Byrnes, Fitzgeralds, Nagles and O'Gormans, and others too, had intermarried. A generation of their menfolk had bonded in the War of Independence and the Civil War. Many of the men had availed of the sexual favours of Moll McCarthy, and at least two in the immediate vicinity had fathered children by her. She was a social embarrassment, as were her children.

Crucially Moll's association with Sergeant Anthony Daly – whatever form it took – brought a real and immediate risk for the Old IRA men in the neighbourhood, heightened by the search for the abducted Michael Devereux, for whose death George Plant faced a military firing squad in 1942, despite the best efforts of his defence barrister Seán MacBride.

Land was the key to other larger matters. A recent biographer of MacBride, Caoimhe Nic Dháibhéid, put it succinctly: 'Gleeson's position was common enough in rural Ireland throughout the twentieth century: grown men living the lives of adult boys, waiting for their father or uncle to die before they could fully accede to manhood and its attendant privileges of marriage, financial independence or even a room of one's own.'[16] And if men could not marry, then what did they do for sex? The answer was Moll McCarthy and women like her. And then there were women who, without land or money or the promise of it from a father or uncle, would not get married and never have children.

Local people were actively discouraged from giving evidence in Harry Gleeson's favour. The parish priest and his curate declined to do so, and others followed.

Look what the gardaí did to Tommy Reid when he refused to change his story. Look what the IRA did to Michael Devereux, their comrade. For those neighbours who suspected they knew the people who had savagely killed Moll McCarthy, but who let Harry Gleeson take the rap for it, there was another layer of intimidation. The message was quite clear: say nothing or you might be next. If the police don't get you, we will. And so an innocent man was hanged.

Every box, large and small, that could have counted against Gleeson had been ticked: the hostility of the parish priests, Murphy and O'Malley; the fact that south Tipperary was proud of its reputation as an IRA stronghold; Moll's cheerfully brazen defiance of morality in public; the gross misbehaviour of three policemen, Chief Superintendent Edward Reynolds, Superintendent Patrick O'Mahony and Sergeant Anthony Daly; the lack of proof of the time of Moll's death; Judge Martin Maguire's inexperience on the bench; his jealousy toward MacBride (see chapter seven); the jury's hostility to MacBride over his known IRA activities; and the Court of Criminal Appeal's failure to order a retrial when faced with compelling evidence of Maguire's failures as judge.

Added to all these antagonisms was the jury's obvious suspicion that Gleeson had lied in the witness box about not recognising Moll McCarthy's body in the stubble field, and the possibility that he had been much closer to Moll than he had admitted. How could they know where the lies ended and the truth started? Factor in the poisoned relationship between Taoiseach Éamon de Valera and his erstwhile comrades in the IRA, complicated by his necessity to act purposefully against them to preserve his policy of neutrality and keep Ireland out of the Second World War. Men would be hanged, or face a firing squad, to prove that point. Gleeson, although the crime of which he was convicted was not political, was unlucky to be sucked into the backwash of that.

Another unhelpful factor was the speed at which events moved. Moll McCarthy's body was found on 21 November 1940. Harry Gleeson was hanged just five months later, on 23 April 1941. Given the jury's plea for clemency, a reasonable person would be forgiven for believing that the sentence would be commuted to a term of imprisonment and that would allow time for reconsideration to determine if an injustice had been done. All Harry Gleeson had on his side to combat this wall of prejudice was the support of his lawyers and a few faithful friends who believed he was innocent of murder.

On 13 September 2013, the *Irish Independent* reported that a senior counsel[17] had been appointed to carry out an independent review of the conviction of Harry Gleeson, following a submission by the Justice for Harry Gleeson group, led by Seán Delaney and including Tom and Kevin Gleeson, relatives of Harry's, and solicitor Emma Timoney, granddaughter of John Timoney, in cooperation with the Innocence Project at Griffith College Dublin's faculty of law. Thus Harry Gleeson's last words recorded by Seán MacBride are finally coming true: 'I rely on you then to clear my name. I have no confession to make, only that I didn't do it. That is all.'

The simple truth of the matter is this: Moll McCarthy was killed by a group of her neighbours with IRA links. Pak O'Gorman fired the fatal shot, and the conspiracy to murder her involved Jack Nagle, Thomas Hennessy and Paddy Byrne, who suspected she was 'informing' on them to Sergeant Anthony Daly. In the twisted morality of the time, these individuals seem to have convinced themselves that they were performing a public service.

# 7. The Defenders

## SEÁN MACBRIDE

Seán MacBride played an important role in Harry Gleeson's story. As junior counsel for the defence, much of the 'heavy lifting' of preparing for the trial fell on his shoulders and on those of the Caesars' solicitor John Timoney. After Harry Gleeson was interrogated for the second time in four days without legal representation, Bridget Caesar decided to hire a solicitor to represent her husband's nephew. She sent for Timoney from Tipperary town, because there was a family connection. She probably also wanted to avoid using a local man from Cahir or Cashel, with ties to her neighbours' families.

As we have seen, her choice of solicitor did not go down well with Superintendent O'Mahony, who was in charge of the murder investigation. Many people saw his trying to influence the choice of defence solicitor as highly improper behaviour for a senior policeman.

Nearly forty years after the trial, Harry Gleeson's niece Nancy McCarthy of Thurles, County Tipperary, wrote to Seán MacBride asking why, despite the latter's best efforts, her uncle had been hanged.

MacBride's reply to her was considered and kindly phrased:

> I was convinced at the time that Henry Gleeson was innocent of the murder for which he was convicted. Nothing has happened to change my view. You rightly ask why did he get such an unfair trial and why he was not reprieved. The answer involves a combination of a number of different elements, the principal ones of which were:
> 1. That the trial was, in my view, unfairly conducted.
> 2. That the judge, who had himself been a prosecuting counsel, was biased.
> 3. That by reason of the fact that most of the people of New Inn were in some way involved with the late Mary McCarthy, they entered into a conspiracy of silence.

Elsewhere MacBride said that the defence senior counsel James Nolan-Whelan was not in good health at the time of the trial.

He might have added a fourth reason to those he outlined: the name Seán MacBride was anathema to a wide swathe of public opinion in Ireland in the 1940s. For good reasons and bad ones, many had reason to dislike him and all he stood for.

Seán MacBride was – on the face of it – an outstanding choice to act as junior counsel in the defence of Harry Gleeson. Though he had been at the Bar for barely four years, a year earlier he had scored a stunning victory over de Valera's government by blowing a hole in the Offences Against the State Act

Seán MacBride on 1 January 1948, with his party's election manifesto. He would become Minister for External Affairs two months later. COURTESY *THE IRISH TIMES*

of 1939, de Valera's weapon of choice against former IRA men who saw the impending war between Britain and Germany in terms of England's difficulty being Ireland's opportunity.

In the conservative corridors of the Irish legal
system, this son of the glorious revolution – his father
was Major John MacBride, executed for his role in the
1916 Rising, and his mother Maud Gonne MacBride
was a revolutionary and muse to poet William
Butler Yeats – was a breath of fresh air. As a child, he
received his first holy communion from the hands
of Pope Pius X. He had joined the IRA as a teenager
in the aftermath of the 1916 Rising, had opposed the
treaty with Britain, taken part on the republican side
in the Civil War, and risen to be IRA chief of staff in
1936. And now he was pursuing a stellar career as a
lawyer. 'On legal affairs or when speaking to a brief,
he had genius', according to his fellow revolutionary
Peadar O'Donnell.[1]

He would win international honours, the Nobel
Peace Prize in 1974 and the Lenin Peace Prize in 1975
– his detractors derived amusement from the con-
junction of Lenin and peace – and served as Minister
for External Affairs between 1948 and 1951.

Then, as now, he was a deeply polarising figure.
'His contribution to the cause of peace at home,
to the national debate on the North was in inverse
proportion to his service to peace worldwide', was
Professor John A. Murphy's biting verdict on his
legacy, given in Seanad Éireann on 20 January 1988, a
few days after MacBride's death.

But all this was to come. When Seán MacBride
joined his senior colleague James Nolan-Whelan, a
more experienced but ultimately less distinguished
lawyer, for the defence of Harry Gleeson, along
with a good legal brain and a voracious appetite for
assimilating detail and making sense of it, he had the

following items of personal baggage which would not serve his client well.

1. The judge had a grudge against him. Martin Maguire was hearing his first big case. Previously, as a barrister, Maguire and George Murnaghan, junior counsel on the prosecution side, had been on the losing side to MacBride a year earlier in the *habeas corpus* case which upset the Offences Against the State Act 1939, mentioned above. That a relative newcomer to the Bar, not yet a senior counsel, had inflicted such a humiliation on established members of the profession was not to be forgotten.

2. The jury was not well disposed towards him. The stoutly middle-class jury knew of MacBride and his revolutionary politics, and disapproved of them. Solid middle-class citizens are not easily won over by former gunmen.

3. His accent counted against him. MacBride's first language was French, and his English was heavily accented. In addition, he spoke with a lisp. Some of his pronunciations of English words were simply hard to follow. There were very few foreigners in Ireland in the 1930s and 1940s and little tolerance for any departure from Irish norms of speech and behaviour. It was too easy to take a dislike to him. Many have told me of MacBride's personal warmth and charisma; however, a trial in which a man faced the death sentence is not a forum where these characteristics were likely to come to the fore.

4. In the background, there was also bad blood between MacBride and senior garda officers over

IRA activities in which MacBride had played a leading role. Chief Superintendent Edward Reynolds had clashed with MacBride over a highly combustible IRA–Blueshirt confrontation in Limerick on 24 September 1933. Cumann na nGaedheal leaders Eoin O'Duffy, W. T. Cosgrave and James Dillon were attempting to address an open-air meeting. Reynolds, then a superintendent, reckoned there were 1,500 potential combatants in the area, and he had only 400 policemen to deal with them. The IRA attacked the platform, the Blueshirts fought back, the gardaí waded in and the IRA withdrew to enjoy the spectacle of those who supported law and order fighting with the forces of law and order. Some thirty-three people were hospitalised. Senior officers like Reynolds knew that they were dancing at the end of strings being pulled by MacBride and his friends, and they did not like it.

5.  MacBride's half-sister Iseult was married to Francis Stuart, who was known to be in Berlin, the capital of Hitler's Third Reich, working as an academic, having gone there bearing a message from IRA leaders MacBride, Stephen Hayes (then IRA chief of staff) and Jim O'Donovan (the IRA master bomber) as the war between Britain and Germany got under way. This caused some people to wonder where MacBride's loyalties really lay.

In later life, MacBride would say that his opposition to capital punishment was based in part on the hanging of Harry Gleeson. In earlier times, he appears to have been less troubled by the loss of human life. On 14

March 1921, he took part in the 'Battle of Brunswick Street' between B Company of the Dublin Brigade of the IRA on one side, and the Dublin Metropolitan Police and Crown forces on the other. This followed the hanging of six republicans in Mountjoy Jail that morning. This was, in effect, an IRA ambush, and seven people died as a result of it, including two police constables, two Auxiliaries, and MacBride's fellow IRA officer Leo Fitzgerald. It fell to MacBride to break the news to Fitzgerald's family and to attend the funeral.

This and other exploits brought MacBride to the notice of Michael Collins and he was charged with raising the revolutionary temperature in County Wicklow by attacking police stations as the prospect of a truce became greater.

In his memoir, *That Day's Struggle*[2] MacBride reflected on IRA courts martial – often of people who had served with the British military – with some distaste. 'I think that probably many people were executed as result of this kind of drumhead court martial who probably should not have been executed and shot by the IRA.' However, this distaste did not stop him from taking the positions of adjutant general, director of intelligence and, briefly in 1936, chief of staff of the IRA when the incumbent Moss Twomey was jailed. However, by the end of the 1930s, MacBride had moved from IRA activism to being 'standing counsel' for republicans before the courts, having made his first court appearance in December 1937.

The *habeas corpus* case cast a shadow over the Harry Gleeson trial to an extent that has not been fully understood. That shadow included the problem of keeping IRA supporters from declaring for Germany in the war that had just started, de Valera's difficulty in facing down people who had helped to put him in power, and the practical impossibility of enforcing law and order without jettisoning civil liberties.

Just a year before Moll McCarthy was murdered, on 17 November 1939, MacBride applied for a writ of *habeas corpus* (effectively the release) for Seamus Burke, a Mayo IRA man who had been arrested under the Offences Against the State Act of 1939 and held in Arbour Hill prison since September. MacBride contested the provision in the Act which allowed a Cabinet minister who is satisfied that a person is acting against the preservation of peace order or security of the State to order the detention of such a person. After some skirmishing involving the choice of judge to hear his application, MacBride won a famous victory. Judge Gavan Duffy granted an order releasing the prisoner, saying: 'the power to intern on suspicion or without trial is fundamentally inconsistent with the rule of law.'

In effect, this was the first successful legal test of the 1937 Constitution and represented a significant achievement for MacBride. The *habeas corpus* case verdict was a setback to government efforts to scupper the IRA's 'England campaign' – bombing strategic targets in Britain – just as the Second World War began, and imperilled the Irish strategy of neutrality. Moreover, while de Valera and his Minister for Justice, Gerald Boland, were trying to pursue a hard anti-IRA line at home, it was somewhat uncomfortably pleading for clemency from Britain for IRA bombers Peter Barnes and James McCormick, who had killed five people in the English city of Coventry on 25

August 1939. The pleas failed and the two men were hanged on 7 February 1940. But the mixed message had gone out: the de Valera government could be two-faced in dealing with the IRA.

The flawed sections of the Offences Against the State Act would be quickly amended by emergency legislation, and MacBride's *habeas corpus* case victory reversed, but the shock to the legal system caused by his impertinent achievement would not be forgotten.

The McGrath case caused further confusion, albeit of a more political hue. Patrick McGrath was a popular veteran of the Easter Rising and the War of Independence. He was the most prominent of a group of prison hunger strikers protesting against a round-up of IRA suspects in November 1939. A noisy campaign for his release ensued. Eventually, de Valera blinked and McGrath was released 'on health grounds'. McGrath was subsequently arrested and sentenced to death by a military court for the murder of a policeman in 1940. Later, de Valera blamed himself for McGrath's release: 'one of the biggest mistakes I made in my life … had it not been for my action [releasing McGrath in 1939] there would only have been one death, whereas in the event, there were six in all'.[3]

So a little over a year before Harry Gleeson would go on trial for capital murder, two barristers who would have a profound effect on his fate locked horns in court over IRA activities. On one side was Seán MacBride and against him was the more experienced Martin Maguire, acting for the attorney general in resisting the release of IRA man Seamus Burke.

Now newly elevated to the High Court bench, Martin Maguire's first major murder trial would be that of Henry Gleeson, and it is clear from the trial transcript that he had not adjusted to being an impartial judge. At times, his interventions against the accused and his legal team indicate that he thought he was still a prosecutor. And, perhaps more importantly, he had a chance to turn the tables on the upstart MacBride.

There is also a serious question to be asked about Nolan-Whelan and MacBride's handling of the case. Was the wrong defence mounted? MacBride always maintained that Gleeson's was the only non-political capital case he took on at the time. And he was paid for his services in the Gleeson case, while he refused payment for his IRA cases. Yet, with his IRA background, he must have known about the activities of veteran republicans Thomas Hennessy and Jack Nagle, among others. What if they had been cross-examined about the earlier arson attack on Moll McCarthy's cottage? For whatever reasons, Gleeson's defence team eschewed the tactic of showing that others had an interest in silencing Moll, and challenging their testimony, in favour of a 'challenge to the prosecution to prove its case' defence which – in the event – failed.

It would have been interesting to hear Super-intendent Patrick O'Mahony cross-examined on his dealings with Thomas Hennessy, once his sworn enemy, now his 'sword-carrier' in the Local Defence Force. In the end, the choice of how to defend a client is one his legal team must make based on the realities of the time. But the notion that they did not recognise the political aspects of this trial now looks far-fetched.

That MacBride made the political connection is clear from his file on the Gleeson case. It contains a copy of what appear to be draft terms of reference for an official inquiry into Stephen Hayes' 'confession' and the circumstances of the death of Seán Russell, an IRA chief of staff who died on a German U-boat travelling to Ireland in August 1940.

## Terms of Reference

To enquire into whether the Government or any of its agents were in touch with Stephen Hayes, Laurence de Lacy or any of their agents, and whether the Government or any of its agents directed or had prior knowledge of activities carried out by the IRA and to inquire into the circumstances surrounding the death of Seán Russell.[4]

## Personnel of Inquiry

Any three responsible persons acceptable to the government and the IRA jointly.

With the draft is a list of questions to be put to the government. Clearly this document is evidence that MacBride was acting for the IRA in some kind of negotiation with the authorities. Most of the points concern Russell, but three focus on Michael Devereux.

When did the government first become aware that Devereux had disappeared?

When and how did the government ... become aware that he had died?

When and how did the government ... become aware of the location of Devereux's body and car?

The significance of Devereux's name occurring in MacBride's Gleeson file is this: it makes a direct connection between MacBride, the search for Devereux and the trial of Harry Gleeson. This came about because the Northern command of the IRA, having earlier had problems of its own with informers, was now convinced that the organisation south of the border was riddled with informers. This had prompted the abduction of Michael Devereux, an IRA man from Wexford, his murder by George Plant and the concealment of his body.

The manner in which the gardaí contrived this catastrophic fratricide within the IRA is instructive. Someone, probably a detective called Denis (Dinny) O'Brien, was keeping a very close eye on IRA activities. O'Brien was a former IRA man, who had fought on the anti-Treaty side in the Civil War, but had joined the police in 1933 and proved remarkably effective as a detective in tracking down former comrades. He noticed that Michael Devereux, a 24-year-old IRA quartermaster and petrol-tanker driver from County Wexford, was meeting other IRA suspects at 22 Lansdowne Road, Dublin. O'Brien was also aware of the location of arms dumps in County Wexford, but decided to keep that information to himself until he was ready to use it. Devereux was arrested, and held in prison. The detective saw to it that word got back to the IRA leadership, via prisoners especially released for that purpose, that Devereux 'was singing like a songbird' in prison. Soon afterwards, Devereux was released, and within days the arms dumps were raided, providing 'proof positive' to the IRA that he had informed on his comrades to secure his release.

Three IRA men – George Plant, Paddy Davern and Michael Walsh – were given orders to deal with Devereux. They successfully persuaded him that he was in danger, and to go 'on the run' with them, initially staying in a safe house in Grangemockler, County Tipperary. On their way to another safe house, Plant pulled out a gun, accused Devereux of being an informer and shot him. Devereux was dead before Moll McCarthy died, but the manhunt continued because his body was not found for eighteen months, almost six months after Gleeson was hanged.

IRA paranoia – again skilfully stoked by the gardaí – now dictated that its chief of staff, Stephen Hayes, be court-martialled. The worried Northern leadership of the IRA was having second thoughts and decided that perhaps Devereux was not an informer, but that Stephen Hayes, also from County Wexford, was. Hayes was duly 'arrested' by IRA heavies. While being held in IRA custody in a house in the Dublin suburb of Rathmines, Hayes began writing a 'confession' detailing his treachery, and implicating government ministers James Ryan and Thomas Derrig, filling page upon foolscap page with fanciful ramblings. Historian Caoimhe Nic Dháibhéid neatly describes the confession as 'an interminable imaginative arabesque'.[5]

The IRA leadership was puzzled by the unfolding 'confession' and asked MacBride for his advice on how to handle this material, which chimed with their worst imaginings. MacBride provided a stock IRA response by seeing the hand of British intelligence in the matter, but the delay served Hayes' purpose, buying him time until he managed to jump out of the window of the suburban house in which he was being held, and run around the corner to the police station, seeking protection from his own subordinates.

When Devereux's body was found shortly afterwards,[6] buried under stones on the mountains between Tipperary and Waterford, it confirmed to the IRA that Hayes had told gardaí where to find the body. Here, then, was the proof that Hayes was the informer they thought he was. But it is possible to read those events the other way around. Hayes was not an informer but the victim of misplaced paranoia. He pulled the wool over his jailers' eyes and escaped with his life. Devereux was less lucky. He did not even have the pretence of a court martial, and was summarily executed. Many now believe that Devereux did not inform on his comrades.

The significance for Harry Gleeson's fate is twofold:

1. MacBride's file on Gleeson clearly linked the Devereux disappearance with the Moll McCarthy murder. The cache of significant IRA-related documents found within the MacBride file on the Gleeson case goes beyond the possibility of simple misfiling. However, MacBride maintained that the Gleeson case was not a political one.

2. The Devereux manhunt had brought unwelcome pressure on those in New Inn and elsewhere who had joined the Local Defence Force as a way of getting back onside with the authorities. Sergeant Anthony Daly was taking a close interest in 'safe houses' in the area to see if Devereux was being sheltered in

one there or thereabouts. And Moll McCarthy
was far too well connected to Anthony Daly
for any of those people to sleep comfortably in
their beds at night.

The draft of the agreement on an inquiry is undated,
and the assumption is that Seán MacBride was trying
to negotiate with Éamon de Valera, with whom he
had a line of communication, in the wake of Stephen
Hayes' 'confession'. There is no sign that de Valera
considered this offer. Further evidence of how well
connected MacBride was at this time is found in a copy
of a handwritten letter to Gerald Boland, Minister
for Justice. Written on 11 April 1941 – and beginning
'Dear Gerry' – MacBride sent him his own personal
copies of the statements of additional witnesses
John Timoney had located, and says that others who
could have come forward would not, because they
did not want to be 'dragged into the case'. Placing
great emphasis on new evidence about shots heard,
MacBride told the minister that he would receive an
official memo on the case from Nolan-Whelan and
himself after the Easter weekend.

The existence of this channel of communication
gives the lie to Marcus Bourke's suggestion that
Peter Berry, Boland's private secretary, dismissed
such evidence without reference to his minister.
And it tends to reinforce the commonly held belief
that Boland himself – despite taking a hard line on
refusing pardons to others condemned to death – was
open to persuasion in this case, but that his Taoiseach
was not for turning.

MacBride's file on the defence of Harry Gleeson at
the Central Criminal Court in February 1941 clearly

shows that he conducted very detailed research into the law and the facts of the case. The accusation made by some that his mind was elsewhere on weightier matters of state and subversion does not stand up. His detailed analysis of which witness said what shows that his thought processes owe much to mathematics – this he shares with his old adversary Éamon de Valera. His correspondence with Harry Gleeson's family and friends throughout is conducted with old-fashioned courtesy and respect for their ordeal. The painful honesty with which Harry Gleeson conducted his final interview with MacBride, on the eve of his hanging, show the condemned man's liking and respect for his lawyer. MacBride kept his note of that conversation all his life, and Harry Gleeson's final words in the condemned cell in Mountjoy Jail still ring true three-quarters of a century later: 'I rely on you then to clear my name.'

A rounded verdict on MacBride's role in Harry Gleeson's defence might pick some holes in his performance as a lawyer, but note that more important factors came into play and affected the outcome – including his background of IRA activism, added to the jealousy of his colleagues, neither of which did his client any favours.

Later, Seán MacBride defended George Plant when he was charged with the murder of Michael Devereux. The criminal trial collapsed for lack of evidence. A court martial followed with less stringent evidence requirements and Plant was executed by firing squad. Plant's family was not told of this until after the event, and this aspect caused widespread revulsion.

On the morning of 9 September 1942, Sergeant Dinny O'Brien was leaving his home near Rathfarnham in Dublin when he was cut down by machine-gun fire. IRA man Charlie Kerins was hanged for O'Brien's murder on 1 December 1944. George Plant's remains were initially buried in Portlaoise prison grounds but later reinterred in a churchyard in his home, St Johnstone, County Tipperary, with IRA military honours. George Plant's memory is revered in parts of Tipperary to this day. For Dinny O'Brien's service to the Irish nation, I can find no memorial.

## JOHN J. TIMONEY

*by Emma Timoney*

My grandfather John Timoney was a constant presence in my family's life. That he was a solicitor with a passion for justice, that he had been a Dáil deputy from 1948 to 1951, and that he had died young – long before his life's work was done, long before I was born – all this I knew. I admired him hugely and I chose law as a career because of him, but I had very little detail of his life and did not like to ask too many questions: my father, also named John, was very young when his father died and might have been upset by being asked to revisit a painful period in his life.

There is no doubt in my mind that my grandfather's death at such a young age had a huge impact on my father's life and I often wonder how different things would have been if he had not suffered the massive heart attack that led to his death in 1961, when my father was only fourteen, leaving behind a wife and four children.

Growing up in Clonmel, I first heard of my grandfather's involvement in the Harry Gleeson trial in 1993 when Marcus Bourke published his account of events. I was just ten or so, but can remember being mesmerised by the story, and by my grandfather's part in it. It always stayed in the back of my mind as something that I had to know more about and when the opportunity arose to become involved in this book, I was delighted that someone with a better ability to investigate the story than I shared my interest. However, this also brought me up against the fact that, though I was inspired to study law by his example, I knew very little detail about my grandfather.

I had not known that my grandfather John Timoney, in addition to being Harry Gleeson's solicitor, was related to some of the people involved in the case. John Timoney was a cousin of Dolly Furlong, whose husband Pat was one of Harry's closest friends, and this meant that he was a cousin of Tim Godfrey who campaigned for a pardon for Harry after Marcus Bourke's book was published. John Timoney was also the Godfrey family solicitor, as well as being a family friend. When Harry Gleeson was hanged, my grandfather continued to protest that he was innocent, and this continued until his death.

People who knew my grandfather always comment on his honesty and straight nature. He was a man who thrived on justice and that was clearly carried through in his choice of career.

John J. Timoney. COURTESY EMMA TIMONEY

My grandfather's firm was taken over when he died and, unfortunately, as so many years have passed since the events of 1940, his file on the case has been destroyed.

John's father, my great-grandfather, was James Timoney, a substantial shopkeeper in Cappawhite,

County Tipperary. He was an active member of Muintir na Tíre, with community development being his passion, particularly vocational education. He had a great interest in politics and was an unsuccessful Fine Gael candidate in the 1937 general election. He, too, was a powerful man. He had to be, because his wife died during childbirth, leaving him to look after the family business as well as a newborn child. He later remarried but had no more children. His only son John was educated at Mount St Joseph College in Roscrea and studied law at University College Dublin.

I cannot say when John J. Timoney and Seán MacBride's paths first crossed, but it is clear that working together on Harry Gleeson's defence in 1940–41 cemented the bond between them and led to my grandfather's involvement in MacBride's new party, culminating in his election to the Dáil in 1948.

On 10 January 1948, the *Tipperary Star* reported on the selection of two Clann na Poblachta candidates for the South Tipperary constituency: a national school teacher, Seán Murray of Killenaule, and solicitor John Timoney of Tipperary town; another candidate was already in the field. 'Mr Timoney is a son of Mr James Timoney of Cappawhite, for many years a well-known figure in the public life of south Tipperary, being a member of the county council for a period of years.' John Timoney had been an active member of Clann na Poblachta in a recent by-election, and he held an LLB degree, readers were told.

At the hustings in his hometown in January 1948, John Timoney spoke plainly. Clann na Poblachta 'had no use for vituperation, mud-slinging or abuse'. Fianna Fáil had been calling him and his colleagues communists, he said in a speech reported by the

*Clonmel Nationalist.* 'De Valera had only recently denounced the practice of making false accusations. Why does he not put a muzzle on one of his ministers whose chief claim to notoriety is his aptitude for mud-slinging?' Timoney went on to deny being a communist, saying he and his colleagues were Christians, and their economic and social policies were based on papal teaching.

On 7 February, the *Tipperary Star* had the early election results. Dan Breen and Michael Davern headed the poll for Fianna Fáil, with Fine Gael's leader, General Richard Mulcahy, a close third. Outgoing Fianna Fáil TD Frank Loughman had nearly 4,000 votes, while John Timoney was in sixth position with just under 2,000. Timoney's cause appeared lost – he also had a Clann na Talmhan (a farmers' party) candidate 1,300 votes ahead of him. But the gods of proportional representation smiled on him. His running mates were eliminated, transferring votes to him, and other transfers came his way, and he won the fourth seat in what was a considerable electoral fluke. Outgoing Fianna Fáil TD Frank Loughman could only grit his teeth as what seemed like his safe seat went to the Tipperary solicitor. He would have his revenge by taking back the seat at the next election in 1951.

But, for now, de Valera was ejected from power. As one voter in South Tipperary who resented wartime rationing predicted when spoiling his vote:

> Goodbye de Valera and Seán McEntee
> Who gave us the brown bread and the half-
> ounce of tea
> We are saying goodbye to them all
> As out of the Dáil they must crawl.

General Richard Mulcahy stood aside to allow his colleague John A. Costello to become Taoiseach of a coalition government, with Timoney's party leader Seán MacBride as Minister for External Affairs and a fiery young doctor Noël Browne as Minister for Health. My grandfather, having lost his seat in the 1951 election, returned to his busy legal practice full-time, but he never forgot Harry Gleeson.

Marcus Bourke told a story about the actor Cyril Cusack visiting Tipperary with a touring production sometime in the 1950s. My grandfather and grandmother invited him to a party in his honour, according to a story told by Marcus Bourke. 'Late into the night the visitor asked Timoney what was his most memorable case. Timoney began to tell the story of the Gleeson case … he unfolded the tale of intrigue and silence that he and Seán MacBride had by then almost pieced together.' As my grandfather retold the story about MacBride's last visit to the condemned man, still insisting on his innocence after making his peace with God, John Timoney broke down and wept.

John Timoney died in May 1961, and his law practice was taken over by Brendan Jones.

*Emma Timoney is a solicitor who practices in Clonmel, County Tipperary.*

# Epilogue

## *Harry Gleeson pardoned in 2015*

Times change, and there is now a greater awareness of miscarriages of justice and a willingness to address them. In 2012, Seán Delaney, a retired man living near Thurles, County Tipperary, who knew the background to the case, decided to act on his belief that Gleeson was innocent. He convened a meeting, including members of the Gleeson family, which led to the formation of the Justice for Harry Gleeson group, to campaign for a pardon. The group made contact with the Innocence Project at the law faculty of Griffith College, Dublin, led by its dean, David Langwallner.

The Irish Innocence Project is part of a global organisation of the same name. It was established in Ireland in 2009 with the mandate of unearthing new facts in cases where there is a belief that a miscarriage of justice has taken place, and is staffed by law students and their teachers. The Innocence Project, drawing on the work done by the Justice for Harry Gleeson group and previous researchers, compiled a dossier which it submitted to the then Minister for Justice Alan Shatter who referred it to senior counsel Shane Murphy for his opinion.

In January 2015 it was announced that Gleeson would receive a posthumous pardon. Thus Gleeson's plea to Seán MacBride on the eve of his death has finally been dealt with: 'The last thing I want to say is that I will pray tomorrow that whoever did it will be discovered and that the whole thing will be like an open book.'

Harry Gleeson has been finally vindicated, but the other victim in this dreadful tale has not. Moll McCarthy tried to fend for herself and her children as best she could and lost her life in dreadful circumstances.

We must remember the injustice done to her.

An undated photograph of Harry Gleeson. COURTESY TOM GLEESON

*I rely on you then to clear my name. I have no confession to make, only that I didn't do it. That is all. I will pray for you and be with you if I can whenever you … are fighting and battling for justice.*

Last words of Harry Gleeson to
Seán MacBride, 22 April 1941.

# Appendix: Portraying the Story in Literature and on Screen

Although the case of Moll McCarthy and Harry Gleeson never resurfaced in the courts after 1941, and was little discussed outside Tipperary, it has fascinated a diverse group of writers and programme-makers. Some had a direct connection to events in Marlhill in November 1940; others simply made use of the dramatic events for their own purposes, often leaving the reader in the dark about how and where the story had begun.

Popular novelist Una Troy was one of these writers. In Irish terms, she might be described as the Maeve Binchy of the 1950s. Her interest in Moll McCarthy started when Una was a sixteen-year-old schoolgirl sitting on the public benches at Cashel district court one fine day around 1926. She was a bookish girl with an enquiring mind, and had already written poetry, now in the possession of the National Library of Ireland.

Her father, District Justice Seán Troy, was on the bench. The gardaí were seeking a court order for the

committal to state care of the children of one Moll
McCarthy of Marlhill, New Inn. She was stated to be
an unmarried mother living in a very dilapidated two-
room cottage, breeding greyhounds for a living, and
was incapable of looking after her growing family.
Judge Troy noticed that two of her children were in
court, and he called them up to question them. Before
long, the judge had established that the children were
well fed and looked after, and he dismissed the case.

Some thirty years later, Una Troy's *We Are Seven*
was published. A novel, it tells the story of Bridget
Monaghan, who was apprenticed to a dressmaker.
When her father died suddenly, Bridget returned
home with a baby, but no husband, and she went on
to have five more children by different men, and even
had the nerve to call the youngest boy Pius after the
then pope. (This was quite a daring joke for an Irish
writer in the 1950s.) The problem for her neighbours
was aggravated by the fact that although the boys got
into scrapes, the happiest family for miles around was
Bridget Monaghan's brood. 'The devil looks after his
own,' some muttered darkly. Una Troy had adapted
aspects of the early life of Moll McCarthy to construct
a romantic fiction celebrating the achievement of an
unconventional woman.

In the intervening years, between sitting in court
and watching her father refusing to break up a
relatively contented family – it would take murder
to achieve that – Una Troy wrote almost twenty
novels. In the 1930s and 1940s, she wrote as Elizabeth
Connors, adapting her work for the stage, and began
publishing under her maiden name in the 1950s.
Many of her books were published in the United

States, and some were translated into German. She had a nice light touch as a storyteller.

Very few of Una Troy's readers would have known that in *We Are Seven* she was describing real events, albeit in a romanticised format. She is clearly enjoying herself, poking fun at her father and the respectable matrons of the village of Doon, her name for New Inn, in chapter three. The women want Bridget Monaghan moved out of the parish, and have persuaded the gardaí to seek a court order committing the children to the orphanage on the grounds that they are being neglected.

Bridget Monaghan and her brood turn up for the hearing in a hired car, further inflaming the community's scandalised respectable women. The entire village had turned out for the case, the most exciting event that ever happened in Doon.

Here Una Troy describes her father, the judge:

> It was unfortunate for those most deeply inter-
> ested in the *Monaghan* case that their district
> justice had a sense of humour. All day through
> [hearing cases of] drunks and pickpockets, he
> had been looking forward to the Monaghans:
> now that they were before him, he was not
> disappointed.
>
> He heard the evidence of a Society for the
> Prevention of Cruelty to Children inspector,
> remarking: 'They look well nourished, Inspector.'
>
> The inspector says the family income is very
> small, mainly from dressmaking. The eldest
> daughter Mary interjects, 'Mother is a good
> manager. And Tommy – that's my brother – he
> brings his wages home every week.'

The judge was already inclined to think that it was this quiet handsome girl who was the good manager. He said to the inspector: 'We can ask them. That's often the most satisfactory solution, don't you think?' (He didn't and neither did the inspector, but the judge was enjoying himself immensely.)

'Are you well fed, children?'

'No,' said Toughy. [Toughy is a ragamuffin, probably ten years old – he is five when the reader first meets him. He clearly is a Celtic cousin of Richmal Crompton's unruly hero in *Just William*.]

'Indeed?' said the judge.

'One spoon of jam each at tea. That's not well fed.'

'You seem healthy enough on it,' the judge said gravely.

'Oh I'm healthy, but it's not well fed. Fed but not well fed.'

The judge changed tack. 'The house is clean and neat?'

The [Society for the Prevention of Cruelty to Children] inspector agreed grudgingly.

'And the children are certainly clean?'

Again Toughy spoke. 'I'm not always as clean as this. That's because they washed me before I came. I'm often dirty, very dirty.'

The judge says he can only go by the evidence before him.

The inspector tried one final ploy.

'I think the fact of their being there proves that the mother is unfit to have care of the children.'

'I have heard no evidence against the children's character so far.'

None was forthcoming and the judge dismissed the application to take the children into care.

'In God's name,' the judge asked the garda sergeant later, 'why was that application brought?'

'Pressure,' replied the sergeant philosophically.

'Yes, I suppose there would be pressure.' The judge laughed but he was angry too. He objected to the attempt to make him a tool to eradicate the consequences of erring respectability. 'They're nice children.'

'They are all right,' said the sergeant. 'The only thing anyone has against them is that they shouldn't be there at all.'

Here Una Troy is treading a path between fact and fiction, between comedy and tragedy. When she writes about the judge, her father in real life, the essentials cannot be other than true, though details diverge. There's a nice tribute to Moll's eldest daughter, Mary, in real life in the way Una Troy describes Mary Monaghan, Bridget's eldest and the role she played in keeping the fictional family together.

Though light, *We Are Seven* bears reading today. Troy had a cool, observant eye. Elsewhere, of a firm of fictional estate agents in Waterford, Sampson and Walsh, she writes: 'It employed three male clerks and five female typists. Three of the typists were plain and efficient, of the remaining two one was pretty, one was very pretty and both slightly less efficient. The plain ones were engaged by Mr Sampson, who had long noted the diminishing correlation between comeliness and competence...' This has to be from life.

But this truncated version of Moll's story was destined for an even wider audience. Elstree Studios – not Hollywood but almost the next best thing – beckoned. Renamed *She Didn't Say No*, it was made into a film and was the British entry in the Brussels film festival in 1958. There were protests before and after the film was made. Filming was switched from Ireland to the south-west of England as a result of hostility to the subject matter – an unmarried woman bringing up six illegitimate children in rural Ireland. Actor Cyril Cusack refused a part in it. Most leading parts were played by English or Scottish actors, but Jack MacGowran, Ray McAnally, Anna Manahan and Hilton Edwards had supporting roles.

As the date of the film's release approached, a further bout of humbug arose, egged on by what was effectively Ireland's first tabloid newspaper, the *Sunday Review*, and aided by the British-based *Empire News*. Both campaigned against the film on family-values grounds. The reality of the underlying real attack on family values by Irish society was completely lost on these crusaders for truth and justice.

A pained correspondence ensued between Una Troy and an official in the Department of External Affairs. She complained that the Irish ambassador in Brussels was lobbying against the inclusion in the Brussels Film Festival of *She Didn't Say No*, which she had co-written, when the ambassador clearly had not seen the film. An official in Dublin, one Conor Cruise O'Brien, replied lamely: 'The Irish minister [diplomat] in Brussels had no advance notice of the showing of the film in question and did not attend the showing. He learned of its nature and setting in Ireland only after its presentation in newspaper reports.' Cruise O'Brien – soon to leave the civil service to play a prominent role in Irish politics – continued: 'As it was apparent on the basis of these reports that the film would be the occasion of harmful publicity to Ireland, he was instructed to draw that fact to the attention of the appropriate authorities.'

Meanwhile, Tipperary Fianna Fáil TD Frank Loughman urged the Department of Foreign Affairs to tell Britain to withdraw the film from the Brussels festival, because it would bring bad publicity on Britain too. The British reply to this patent nonsense was to say that the choice of the film was a matter for the British film industry, not Her Majesty's government, so it was unable to help. Loughman, a pharmacist from Clonmel, represented Tipperary constituencies in the Dáil between 1938 and 1961, with intervals spent in the Senate. According to Marcus Bourke, Loughman was a friend of the former parish priest of New Inn and former IRA man Father Edward Murphy, and knew Thomas Hennessy and Jack Nagle well.[1] Loughman understood the Moll McCarthy murder case background fully. One can only guess at the convolutions his conscience went through to describe these events as a blemish on Britain's reputation.

I like to think that Una Troy, in writing *We Are Seven*, was not just concocting a light-hearted romance. She was saying something important about families and telling the world that Moll McCarthy –

whatever else she was – deserved credit for trying to be a good mother to her children, and that while women may find men attractive, in the long run they are not always essential.

Una Troy married a doctor called Joseph Walsh. She died in Waterford in 1993.

Other authors have drawn on the story of Moll and Harry. Undoubtedly the most readable version is Carlo Gébler's novel *The Dead Eight*, published in 2011. Gébler sets real events in New Inn in 1940 in thriller form, adding little to the plot, apart from fleshing out the story with fictional details to smooth out the narrative. The book can be read on two levels: simply as a fast-moving thriller, or as a means of getting a closer understanding of what really happened. Perhaps both. The 'dead eight' of the title of Gébler's work refers to a double-barrelled shotgun, and one is featured on the cover. Bourke had contacted Gébler – having read a previous work by him based on fact. This was in the aftermath of the publication of *Murder at Marlhill*, when Marcus Bourke was hoping to kindle further interest in the case.

Evelyn Conlon's novel *Skin of Dreams* looks at how lives can be affected by the discovery of a secret. A woman clearing out her late parents' home finds that a relative was hanged in the 1940s. It becomes obvious to her that the man was innocent, but she does not share this knowledge with her twin brother. The plot owes much to the fate of Harry and Moll, but it is not their story.

However, as we have already seen, the first writer in the field was Maurice Walsh, author of 'The Quiet Man'. Walsh was from Lisselton in north Kerry, and the University of Limerick acquired some of his papers in 2000. They contain correspondence from David Sears, an *Irish Independent* court reporter who attended the murder trial of Harry Gleeson. Walsh and Sears did not just adopt the medical evidence and the crime scene and turn it to their own purpose. In constructing a fiction about a miscarriage of justice, they identified the two major fault lines in the Gleeson trial: the inability of the prosecution to identify the time of death, and the accused's lies, which caused the jury to doubt all that he said, even when it should have been clear that he was telling the truth.

While I was working on this book, a colleague sent me a cutting from a south London newspaper, the *Southwark News*, reporting that Michael McCarthy had been beaten to death. One of Michael's eleven or twelve children, Francis, aged forty-three, was suffering from mental problems when he killed his father in Chatham Street, Walworth, south London, on 12 April 2003. They had fallen out because Michael, then aged seventy-four, had tried to evict his son, who claimed that he had redecorated the house but had not been paid for his work. Matters came to a head when Michael bought a new settee with cash when Francis wanted him to get it on credit. Francis wanted the cash for drink and drugs and he lost all patience with the old man and beat him to death with a claw hammer. The previous day, he had told his brother Anthony, 'Dad's doing my fucking head in. If he carries on, I'm going to kill him.'

The following day, Francis McCarthy went to the local police station and confessed that he had killed his father. He accompanied the police to the house where Michael lay dead on the settee. He pleaded guilty to manslaughter on the grounds of diminished responsibility and was jailed indefinitely later in 2003 under the Mental Health Act. I understand that Patrick McCarthy died some years ago, and I have no knowledge of the whereabouts of Moll McCarthy's three younger children.

# Endnotes

## Chapter 1: South Tipperary in 1940

1  Mary Carr (ed.) *Knockgraffon School 1871–1992*. The contributor quoted is Bridget Egan.
2  Most accounts say Anastasia Cooney was a nurse. Her grandniece Carmel O'Leary has a collection of her papers in a folder bearing the crest of the Queen Alexandra Imperial Nursing Service, to which she either belonged or with which she worked closely. Not all female ambulance drivers had been trained as nurses, but it is likely that Anastasia Cooney did her nursing for the Order of St John of Jerusalem, better known today as the Order of Malta.
3  According to Carmel O'Leary, Margaret's (Peggy's) body was taken away at Anastasia Cooney's behest and buried in a graveyard in Kilsheelan. However, popular belief in New Inn to this day is that Moll is buried in Garranlea, in a small private graveyard close to the Cooney home, and that Peggy, Moll's last child, is buried there too.

## Chapter 2: A Wicked Murder

1  Members of the Davern family would later play a part in trying to obtain a posthumous pardon for Harry Gleeson.
2  Conversation with Peter Lenehan, 23 July 2013, at Marlhill. He was visiting Ireland from his home in Australia.
3  For clarity: there were two pumps on John Caesar's farm, one in the yard beside the house and another in a field closer to Moll McCarthy's cottage. The water from the field pump tasted brackish in summer, so the yard pump was favoured in the summer months. In November, the field pump water should have been drinkable.
4  Information from campaigners in a more recent miscarriage of justice case.

5 The way in which the matter of the missing sack arose is highly suspect. According to gardaí, Gleeson mentioned it at the end of his first statement, but too late to be included in the version that he signed. Had Gleeson been looking for a particular type of heavy sack used to protect a pump from freezing, he was hardly likely to use it to give Moll potatoes, with winter just beginning.

6 In an exchange of emails with the author in 2013. Dr Marnane is a founder member of the Tipperary Historical Society and familiar with political loyalties in the area.

7 Information given to author by a member of the Byrne-O'Gorman family and partially confirmed by the current owner of the land.

8 The McCarthy children's evidence about times proved to be unreliable. Michael said she went out about 7 p.m.; he probably meant 6 p.m. See also preface re 'new time' and 'old time'.

9 The names of Miss Mary Bridget Cleary, principal teacher of Knockgraffon National School, and Mrs Mary Fitzgerald, assistant teacher, appear in a list of witnesses required by the defence, prepared by John Timoney. It also mentions that the Knockgraffon school attendance book for November 1940 should be produced in court. In the event, neither woman gave evidence and the book was not made available to the court.

10 A neighbour of John Caesar's some years earlier had obtained his land by offering a higher price than a long-time resident of New Inn was prepared to pay. For his trouble, the purchaser was known thereafter in the locality as 'The Grabber'. That nickname was used to refer to him as late as 2014.

## Chapter 3: Trial and Sentence

1 Martin Maguire (1883–1962) was a High Court judge from 1940 to 1954, and a Supreme Court judge from 1954 to 1961. He had qualified as a lawyer in 1911 and become a senior counsel in 1925.

2 James 'Jim' Nolan-Whelan (1883–1950) had a colourful background. He studied law at Oxford and gained a 'double blue' – winning honours for the university at two sports. As a student he had changed his name by deed

poll from Nolan to Nolan-Whelan. He became a barrister in 1904, and senior counsel in 1937. He spent his way through two family fortunes, according to his Law Library colleague Richard Cooke SC.

3  Here Joseph A. McCarthy had combined two statements of Gleeson. The effect is somewhat misleading.

4  This is not correct. The gun was usually kept in Caesar's bedroom, but was left in the kitchen at times when it was in frequent use. Later, Judge Maguire had to correct himself on where the gun was kept.

5  Bill O'Connor writing as 'Ex Creamery Boy' *The Farcical Trial of Harry Gleeson* (privately published, County Tipperary, 1990) pp. 5–6, reproducing report in the *Clonmel Nationalist* dated 4 January 1941.

6  Gleeson's statements to gardaí and his evidence do not ascribe ownership of the greyhound to Scully, or anyone else, but it was widely known in New Inn that Scully owned it, and entrusted it to Gleeson to train.

7  Probably in the 'pump field', close to the McCarthy cottage.

8  See Marcus Bourke, *Murder at Marlhill* (Dublin, 1993), a copy of the school register reproduced at p. 52 shows that Michael McCarthy had attended school on Wednesday, 20 November 1940.

9  There was a conflict between Scully's evidence of who said what, and who was where on that morning in the New Inn garda station, and Daly's account of those events, but it was unimportant in regard to the outcome of the trial.

10  Bill O'Connor, *The Farcical Trial of Harry Gleeson*, p. 78.

11  Garda Ruth had called to Moll's cottage two days earlier about a summons for non-attendance at school.

12  *Murder at Marlhill*, pp. 95–6 and conversation with the author in December 2009.

13  Later this appears as midnight, the difference being accounted for by new time/old time.

14  *The Farcical Trial of Harry Gleeson*, p. 12, contains a report from the Meteorological Office in Dublin on rainfall measured at Clonmel and Cashel, the nearest measurement points – New Inn being at about the midpoint between the two places. On the morning of 20 November at Clonmel, 4 mm of rain was recorded in the previous twenty-four

hours, and 12.2 mm on the morning of 21 November. At Cashel the figures were 1.5mm for 20 November, and 7.3 mm for 21 November. At Birr, fifty miles away, intermittent rain was recorded at night, and overall rainfall exceeded the average for November in both Cashel and Clonmel.

15  The register gives the number as N50686. Gun licences were issued annually and must be produced when buying ammunition. The number for a previous, but by then out-of-date, licence was inserted when the register was 'doctored'. The correct number for that period was P50987 – the author has a copy of that licence.

16  Dr James O'Connor, a kinsman of Bill O'Connor, author of *The Farcical Trial of Harry Gleeson*, appears on the firearms register above an entry for John Caesar on 10 July 1940.

17  Dr John McGrath (1901–1957), graduate in science and medicine, professor of pathology at University College Dublin, State Pathologist 1929–1953.

18  Patrick O'Mahony (1897–1980) joined An Garda Síochána in 1923, was promoted to sergeant in 1924, inspector in 1925, superintendent in 1934, and retired in 1962.

19  MacBride's address is not part of the official court record. He may have meant No. 4 shot, or simply did not understand the difference, nor, I suggest, would the jury.

20  Marcus Bourke spoke to a person who had attended the trial. Bourke would not disclose his name. I believe it was a garda. Be that as it may, this person was sympathetic to Gleeson, and he helped Bourke when he came to write *Murder at Marlhill*. Conversation with the author, 2 December 2009.

21  A man named Aylmer O'Doherty contacted Marcus Bourke after publication of *Murder at Marlhill* was published, saying that he had been in court throughout the Gleeson murder trial. Although Bourke did not identify his witness to the 'cartridge twisting' episode, it was likely to have been a member of the gardaí, on duty during the trial.

22  Since counsels' opening and closing addresses to the jury do not form part of the offical record, what appeared in the press is the only record of what was said. This account is taken from the *Clonmel Nationalist* of 2 March 1941.

23  Reid later sued Chief Superintendent Edward Reynolds and Detective Sergeant James Reynolds, both of Thurles

garda station, for damages arising of an assault in New Inn barracks on 25 November 1940, but he lost his case. Neither garda gave evidence in the Gleeson murder trial.

24  *Murder at Marlhill*, p. 3.

## Chapter 5: Appeal

1  His title was assistant secretary to the government: in modern parlance he would be assistant secretary general to the cabinet. The government would have to give its assent if the death sentence was to be carried out.

2  This appears to bear out Marcus Bourke's contention that Sergeant Anthony Daly was not the only garda of that rank to have had sex with Moll McCarthy.

3  Conversation in June 2012 in Fethard, County Tipperary.

4  *Murder at Marlhill*, p. 69.

5  *The Farcical Trial of Harry Gleeson* pp. 105–8.

6  Abbot Ailbe Sadlier was related to John Timoney: Tim Godfrey letter to Marcus Bourke, 15 June 1995.

7  Telephone conversation with Noel Davern, 5 June 2012.

8  Peter Berry was secretary of the Department of Justice during the Arms Trial in 1970.

9  Note on Department of Taoiseach copy of the Department of Justice circular to ministers dated 8 April 1941, which was subsequently recalled.

10  Department of Justice memorandum to government dated 15 April 1941.

11  Letter from Maguire's private address to Department of Justice, dated 8 April 1941.

12  This is taken from a series of articles in *The Bell* magazine, attributed to prisoner D83222, later revealed to be Walter Mahon-Smith. Writer Seán Ó Faoláin edited *The Bell*, and Dublin 83222 was his phone number. Much of what Mahon-Smith wrote about Gleeson is confirmed by contemporary sources, although he appears to have conflated two hangings, those of Gleeson and of Bernard Kirwan in 1943, about which Brendan Behan wrote in *The Quare Fellow*. Mahon-Smith's articles were published in book form as *I Did Penal Servitude*, by Metropolitan Publishing, Dublin in 1945, and he later became a respected journalist.

13 Gráinne O'Meara, neé Kavanagh, and the author are cousins. She recalled hangings in Mountjoy in the 1940s but not individual ones by name. Her father, Seán Kavanagh, had the distinction of serving as governor in a prison where he had once been held on IRA-related charges.

## Chapter 6: Aftermath

1 Letters from David Sears to Maurice Walsh, Maurice Walsh archive, University of Limerick.
2 The name could be an in-joke. Dublin medical students, of whom McGrath had once been one, were famously fond of drinking in Hartigan's public house in Lower Leeson Street.
3 Bill O'Connor's sister May confirmed this series of events in a phone conversation with the author in May 2014. She said that neither she nor her friend Katie could hear the exchange between Daly and her brother in Barron's public house after the dance.
4 *Sunday Independent*, 8 December 1974.
5 Conversation with the author, October 2009.
6 Marcus Bourke's papers were made available to the author by his son Raymond Bourke.
7 The Irish Sisters of Charity refused to give me any information on Mary McCarthy or to confirm that she had worked at the Magdalene laundry at High Park, Whitehall, Dublin. I believe she did.
8 *Mystery at Marlhill*, RTÉ 1, 23 September 1995.
9 Father James Meehan was a parish priest in New Inn who did intensive research into the murder of Moll McCarthy, according to Marcus Bourke. His researches ended with his death in 1992, and Bourke never succeeded in getting access to his file.
10 *Ceart agus Cóir* was a series of dramatised TV documentaries on capital punishment trials made by independent film company Midas Productions. When this programme was repeated, the accusation against Pak Gorman had been removed, despite the protests of the producer Mike Keane.
11 Document W.S. 1394.

12 Seán Treacy died in 1920 in a shootout with British forces in Talbot Street, Dublin.

13 Tim Godfrey's father, Patrick, and his aunt Dolly were first cousins of solicitor John Timoney. Coincidentally, Dolly's husband, Pat Furlong, was related to John Caesar's second wife, Bridget.

14 In May 2014, following publication of my letter to *The Irish Times* seeking photographs and documents connected with the case, a man living in Cahir contacted me to say that he too had seen the original letter. His recollection of the text confirmed that recorded by Tim Godfrey – even including the 'horrible off-brown notepaper used in the war years'.

15 Bill O'Connor's *The Farcical Trial of Harry Gleeson* is dedicated to Mary Gleeson, who was still alive then and living in America. Marcus Bourke followed suit with the dedication to *Murder at Marlhill*.

16 Caoimhe Nic Dháibhéid, *Seán MacBride: A Republican Life 1904–1946*, Liverpool 2011, p. 162.

17 Shane Murphy SC.

## Chapter 7: The Defenders

1 *The Irish Times*, 6 April 1968.

2 Seán MacBride, Catriona Lawlor (ed.) *That Day's Struggle: a Memoir 1904–1951*, Dublin, 2005, p. 158.

3 *Ibid.*, p. 165.

4 Hayes succeeded Russell as IRA chief of staff – de Lacy was a senior IRA figure whose full-time job was as a journalist on *The Irish Times*.

5 Caoimhe Nic Dháibhéid, *Seán MacBride: A Republican Life 1904–1946*, p. 165.

6 27 September 1941.

## Appendix

1 Conversation with the author, December 2009.

# Acknowledgments

First of all I wish to thank Mary O'Connor, author of *Our Roots Under the Rock*, a history of the extended O'Connor family in south Tipperary and beyond. She gave me the push I needed to stop researching and start writing. Two members of her extended family feature prominently in the story of Harry Gleeson and Moll McCarthy: Dr James O'Connor examined Moll's body at the place where it was found, and Bill O'Connor wrote an angry account of the unfair trial of his friend Harry Gleeson, and, in doing so, gave a lead for others to follow. Seán Olson's enthusiasm, local knowledge and connections encouraged me when my spirits were flagging. Carlo Gébler and Caoimhe Nic Dháibhéid gave great support. And without the help at a critical juncture of Emma Timoney, and more recently of the Jonathan Williams Literary Agency, there simply would have been no book.

Some people specifically asked not to be named. If I have left others out, I apologise and will make amends in any future edition. Those named here may not share my opinions and conclusions; some may dispute them vigorously, and mentioning their courtesy to me does not imply approval on their part. Many others helped in different ways. They include: Mary Aragon, Fiona Aryan, Norbert Bannon, Jonathan Bardon, Ken Bergin, Bernard Boles, the late Marcus Bourke and his son Raymond, Liam Boyd, James Bradbury, Conor Brady, Annette and the late Martin Browne, Paul Buckley, Mairín de Burca, Turtle Bunbury, Ann Butler, Denis Byrne, Father Pat Byrne, Henry Cairns, Tim Carey, Michael Coady, Ann Colbran, Noel Davern, Seán Delaney, John Fitzgerald, Father Denis Foley, Mary Gaughan, Tom and Kevin Gleeson, Patricia and Tom Godfrey, Mary Guinan-Darmody, Willie Hayes, Kevin Healy, Paul Helleris, Matt Hume, Hubert Hume, Joe Joyce, Labhras Joye, Michael Kelleher, Catriona Lawlor, Peter Lenehan, Paul McGarry, Moira MacNamara, Eoin McVey, Anne Markey, Hugh Markey, Dr Denis Marnane, Anne Martin, Tommy Meehan, Senator Paschal Mooney, Des Murnane, Peadar Murnane, Willie and Teresa Nolan, Seán O'Donnell, Liam Ó Duibhir, Father Christy O'Dwyer, Denis and Anne O'Gorman, Kathleen O'Keeffe, Carmel O'Leary, Gerry O'Looney, Fiachra Ó Marcaigh, Gráinne O'Meara, Jim Parkinson, Father Peter Queally, Tom Quinlan, Asta Reddin, Tony Spollen, Peter Stubley, Marilyn and Mervyn Taylor, Elizabeth Verling, Deirdre Vokes-Chrystal, Anne Walsh, Kay Walsh (née O'Connor), John Waters, Tom and Maribel Wood, and members of the Justice for Harry Gleeson group.

I also want to thank my wife Barbara and other members of our family and my friends who have had to live with my preoccupation with these dreadful events.

# Bibliography

Augusteijn, Joost (ed.), *Ireland in the 1930s: New Perspectives.* Four Courts Press, Dublin: 1999.

Bardon, Jonathan, *A History of Ulster.* Blackstaff Press, Belfast: 1992.

Bourke, Marcus (Marcus de Burca), *Murder at Marlhill,* Geography Publications, Dublin: 1993.

Bowyer-Bell, J., *The Secret Army – The IRA 1916–1979.* Poolbeg, Dublin: 1989.

Brady, Conor, *Guardians of the Peace.* Gill & Macmillan, Dublin: 1974.

Carey, Tim, *Mountjoy – The Story of a Prison.* The Collins Press, Cork: 2000.

Carr Mary (ed.), *Knockgraffon School 1871–1992,* privately published, County Tipperary.

Conlon, Evelyn, *Skin of Dreams.* Brandon Books, Dingle, County Kerry: 2003.

Gébler, Carlo, *The Dead Eight.* New Island, Dublin: 2011.

Girvin, Brian, *The Emergency, Neutral Ireland 1939–45.* Macmillan, London: 2006.

Lawlor, Catriona (ed.), *Seán MacBride: That Day's Struggle: A Memoir 1904–1951.* Curragh Press, Dublin: 2005.

Mac Eoin, Uinseann, *The IRA in the Twilight Years – 1923–1948.* Argenta Publications, Dublin: 1997.

Mahon-Smith, Walter, *I Did Penal Servitude by Prisoner D83222.* Metropolitan Publishing, Dublin: 1945.

Mullins, Gerry, *Dublin Nazi No 1,* Liberties Press, Dublin: 2007.

Nic Dháibhéid, Caoimhe, *Seán MacBride: A Republican Life, 1904–1946.* Liverpool University Press: 2011.

O'Connor, Bill, *The Farcical Trial of Harry Gleeson, by Ex Creamery Boy,* privately published, County Tipperary: 1990.

O'Connor, Kevin (ed.), *Thou Shalt Not Kill*, Gill & Macmillan/ RTÉ: 1994.

O'Connor, Mary, *Our Roots Under the Rock*, privately published, Tralee, County Kerry: 2006.

O'Donoghue, David, *The Devil's Deal*. New Island, Dublin: 2010.

Troy, Una, *We Are Seven*, Heinemann, London: 1957.

Walsh, Maurice, *The Man in Brown*, W.R. Chambers, Edinburgh: 1945.

Wood, Tom, *27 Main Street*. Red Hen Publishing, Listowel, County Kerry: 2010.

## Other sources

Sources consulted include: the National Archives of Ireland; National Library of Ireland; Seán MacBride papers courtesy of Catriona Lawlor; Marcus Bourke's papers, Tipperary Studies section, Thurles Library; University of Limerick Special Collections Library; Gilbert Library, Dublin; Dún Laoghaire-Rathdown libraries; Bray Library, County Wicklow; Irish Film Institute archive, Dublin; Military Archives, Dublin; the Garda Museum, Dublin; Blackrock College archives, Dublin; Rockwell College archives, County Tipperary; Southwark borough archives, London; *The Irish Times*; Society of the Divine Word; Colliers undertakers Bray, County Wicklow.

# Index

Note: Illustrations are indicated by page numbers in bold.

# Index

# Index